# DRUIDRY

# DRUIDRY

## EMMA RESTALL ORR

Thorsons

Thorsons
An Imprint of HarperCollins*Publishers*
77–85 Fulham Palace Road
Hammersmith, London W6 8JB

Published by Thorsons 1998

5 7 9 10 8 6 4

A catalogue record for this book
is available from the British Library

ISBN 0 7225 3674 7

Printed and bound in Great Britain by
Caledonian International Book Manufacturing Ltd, Glasgow

# CONTENTS

*This book is offered with sincere and soul-deep thanks to my son Joshua, for his patience and wisdom, and to Philip Shallcrass, for being on so very many occasions my library, filled with information, laughter and affection.*

*I thank too all those in the tradition who spoke to me of their beliefs and practice, and answered my questions with grace and generosity.*

*Hail, my Lord of the Golden Wings, whose flight has carried me through these words! Hail, my Lady of the Sparkling Depths, whose bright darkness showed me the reason why! Hail, blessed ancestors, Druids of Old, may your blessings remain with these words and all who touch them.*

# WHAT IS DRUIDRY?

I f you really want to know, stop reading, just for a while.

*And into a knapsack slip a little food, bread, nuts, an apple or two, whatever you feel you need, and something to drink. Dress for the weather, taking a sweater or a waterproof if necessary. Then stop for a moment. Look around you.*

*And, walking slowly through your home, notice everything that expresses who you are, what you have created, what is in process, what you are hoping to be, or be seen as. Notice what is of value to you and what is not. Choose something which embodies, actually or symbolically, that which you most value, that which has given you the most, allowing you to find the skills and certainty that you know you have. You must be ready to let go of it, to give it away, yet it must mean enough to you for the act of releasing it to be profound, even difficult.*

*Put it into the knapsack or into your pocket and leave the house. Whether by train, car, bicycle or on foot, make your way out of the buildings, the tarmac and concrete, into a landscape that is as close to the wild natural world as you can reach, away from the roads, noise and crowds, away from the fields of sprayed crops and rusting metal.*

*Wherever you find yourself is your own story. It may be on the open moors, with the buzz of bees in the heather and the wind chasing* itself around your clothes. It may be in the forest, with twigs snapping beneath your feet, the smell of leafmould infusing through you. It may be in the park, beneath a willow at a pond's edge, the purring of pigeons lulling you, the city that holds you gently disappearing into calm. We each have a different perception of what is wild and natural (yet safe enough to be in alone). Wherever it is, stay there, for a whole day, or a few days, walking, watching, feeling, sitting, listening – to yourself, to the world around you.

Listening here isn't something that can be done with any effort. It is a process of simply becoming aware, without judgement, without having to react or respond. And as we listen, our bodily senses begin to awake. We start consciously to breathe through our pores, to smell with our skin, to observe and feel with our subtle body of energy. And in doing so, the effects of our presence begin to make less impact on the world around us.

Spend some time listening in this way, and when you stop to eat, share your food, openly and with gratitude, by giving more than a little back to the earth, leaving a pile in a hidden place where it can be found by the little creatures and the faery folk, scattering crumbs over the ground, pouring a good drink into the soil or sand.

When you feel that your presence has begun gently to merge with the environment through which you wander, allow your mind to ponder upon your quest, your desire to know more about the old tradition of Druidry. What is your motivation? What do you hope to gain? What are you expecting? How might it change you? Who would you hope to meet and what would they be like? What would be asked of you?

If you are listening with an open mind, quiet from blending your sense of self with the natural world, the answers that emerge will be your first taste of Druidry. Woven through them will be a clarity that will teach more than any written words. Through them will emerge, too, an understanding of the first step you must take on your journey into the tradition.

*The time has come to leave your gift, both as an offering to the earth which nourishes you and to those who have travelled the path before you, to the Druid ancestors who will guide you upon the way.*

*How the gift is given is up to you. It may be snuggled into the crook of a tree, thrown into water or left at a charity shop on the way home. The nature of the gift and the nature of your world, together with a little common sense and environmental sensitivity, will make the possibilities clear. The important part is the attitude with which it is given, and the letting go.*

*And if you don't find, in honesty, that you have reached a point where you can give your gift, consciously releasing it with thanks, then come back another day, and again and again. But don't read any more, until it is done.*

## THE OLD FELLOW

Somewhere in our minds stands that old Druid we have all taken on board as the original, the prototype. He is slim, around 70, a little under six foot tall, with long white hair, unkempt, and a longer white beard that tapers to a point. He is wearing a simple off-white robe with a long dark cape around his shoulders, the loose folds of a hood, his feet in sandals. In his hand may be a sprig of mistletoe, a golden sickle or an ornate wooden staff.

The details may vary, according to our own intuition as to what characteristics express the qualities he must surely have, but whether a little taller, a little rounder, with dark eyes or blue, he carries aspects of sensitive and powerful older men who have walked through our lives, together with images from storybooks and cartoons we have read, movies we have seen.

Whether he is fair or dark, the old Druid is a source of universal and poignant wisdom. Moving with an otherworldly serenity, he blends gentleness and age with an absolute invulnerability.

For many he seems to be an embodiment of the lands of Britain, Ireland and Brittany, proud with their dignity, rolling hills, wild moors and stormy nights, chaotic like their hedgerows, and as bloody-minded as can be. We sense he could talk with the birds, call up the thunder, stand fearless before any man. Above all, this old Druid who potters around our minds, rubbing his chin and thinking deeply, speaking his truths with a touch of irony, is almost certainly and definitively a 'he'.

## THE REALITY

That archetypal figure even plays his role amongst the growing numbers who practise Druidry today. For a small number the old fellow's image might be a part of the incentive to search out the tradition, firing the imagination, but for many Druids it is what lies beneath the old man's appearance – his strength of spirit, his certainty and flexibility, his connection with the natural world, his sensitivity and wisdom – that is a powerful source of inspiration. Some people might admit to childhood fascinations about Druids awakened by tales of Merlin, Gandalf or Getafix, all of which link into the old wizard wiseman of our collective cultural heritage. And when someone who knows nothing of modern Druidry is told that there are actually Druids still practising the faith today, it is often that image that springs to mind.

Yet when we look at modern Druids, the picture is quite different. We are faced with an enormous range which, as more and more people discover the tradition, is growing ever wider and richer in its variation. The number of Orders and small groups is also growing, each inspired by and expressing a different facet of the tradition, each with different priorities, different spiritual and ritual textures and tones.

The underlying qualities of the old fellow are still there, like a scent in the air, but he is seldom an obvious presence. A Druid now is just as likely to be a woman as a man, and may come from any social, religious or educational background, may have any economic status, be of any sexuality and any race or nationality. People of every age are coming into the tradition, from the children of Druids to the oldest members of society. Urban or rural, the Druid might be an environmental lawyer, a primary school teacher, an art student, a hospital ward sister, an accountant, someone living in a twigloo on a road protest camp or running a computer systems consultancy from Budleigh Salterton or Leeds ...

There is no element of 'evangelism' within Druidry, so that while Druids would hope to live their beliefs with integrity, most would not broadcast the nature of their spirituality. Many work or live alongside colleagues who have no idea that they are practising Druids. So the Druid may be the boss with her laptop, or the lady serving in the cafeteria, or the bloke at goods inwards with the funny moustache, the marketing director who seems so laid back, the photographer at the wedding, the counsellor, the girlfriend's mum ...

These diverse people might celebrate their spirituality in huge open rites or in small private gatherings or joyfully alone. A Druid ceremony might be wild and dramatic, a gathering at night in the depths of the forest, with colour and chanting and drums and firelight, or it might be poignant in the depth of its stillness, thoughtful and precise, in a candlelit room reverberating with the words of old poetry. Modern Druids may also change as they prepare for their rituals, festivals and prayers, the briefcase or toolkit replaced by a harp or chalice, the mind opened wider for the dance of the rite, the everyday suit or jeans laid aside for robes or other special clothes of blue and green, or red and gold, or many colours, often made of undyed natural cloth, some plain, others beautifully ornate.

Whatever the celebration, a key goal is living and breathing the philosophy. So the old fellow who is the Druid archetype of our culture is understood by the lad sitting in a pool of calm, playing upon his harp in a dark green robe beneath the old beech trees, as he is by the woman who meditates before her immaculate altar, sliding into her clearest concept of the perfect light, in a robe of white, edged with violet and red, pondering the problem she has been asked to resolve. Yet what they have both taken from this archetype, consciously or not, to inspire their expression of a spirituality which they both call 'Druidry' might be quite different. What of the priestess with feathers in her hair who walks the moors to an ancient stone circle, chanting to her goddess, laughing with the elves and sprites who run along beside her? She has a connection with the archetype which is different again, as is that of the priest who, in a headdress of antlers, stands at the edge of the field of swaying barley and calls with an Earth-shaking voice to his god of the glorious sun.

From the sage to the mage, the hermit or the court advisor, the wildman of the woods and the village healer, the balladeer and seer, the 'Druid' images held by those now coming into the tradition are almost as varied as the Druids themselves.

So what is it that brings all these people together as active students and celebrants of one tradition? What is Druidry?

## THE LAND BENEATH THE MIST

The areas of common understanding where Druids join together are those which are fundamental to modern Druidry as a whole. It is these that guide the Druid's behaviour, ethics and relationships. When it comes to ritual practice, the common ground is often less obvious, though deeply implicit.

To discover the essence of Druidry we must go far further than the archetype of the old Druid in white with his sparkling eyes, reaching back to the land from which he emerged. Only in journeying to this place can we hope to understand what it is that inspires such a faith to be practised still, with its wealth of individuality, creativity and celebration.

*Druidry is a land that has always existed, yet for thousands of years it has lain beneath a mist. Whether it has ever been without it can only be speculation, a dream memory of the soul. It is a land which knows the mist and is content with it. It is not a comfortable place for an incarnate soul to live, though it is possible to travel there. The mist is not impenetrable, but the journey can be difficult: visibility is often minimal (though at times suddenly and startlingly clear) and there are dangers.*

*If we were to travel to this land from our own, flying perhaps on the back of a merlin falcon, we would be best not to attempt a landing through the mist. However, over the few last millennia, various regions of the land, most often areas of high country, hills and mountains, have broken through the mist. They look, from the merlin's back, like islands in a milky grey sea. The vegetation may be similar, also much of the wildlife, and if we are sensitive enough to feel the energy, the atmosphere, we might believe there to be some ancient connection.*

*When an area does emerge out of the mist, the word spreads amongst those who are interested in this land and it is visited by many people eager to travel through its old forests and meadows, across its moorland and mountains, discovering ancient trackways or creating new ones.*

*Some parts that emerge don't stay clear for long, but disappear beneath the mist again, to be visited only by mystics and madmen.*

*Some areas remain clear for hundreds of years, so that those who visit change the landscape by their presence, taming the wild unknown, making it more accessible for others to follow. Other regions are claimed by those who have visited them and high walls are built as the land is taken into exclusivity. Some are uninhabitable, too high or unstable, but the view of them fills the onlooker with awe.*

*From whichever way you approach this land, wherever you touch your feet upon the Earth, it is not possible to see the whole country. Yet from journeys taken across the different regions that have enjoyed clear air, and from descents made into and through the mist, we can come to an understanding about the nature of the land.*

*Upon this merlin's back, if you will join me, we will catch a glimpse of what lies beneath the mist. And, if you would listen well, while we make our journey, I will speak of what I know to be below that grey and magical sea.*

## THE PROBLEMS WITH FINDING A DEFINITION

Within a spiritual tradition where there are so many different views it is almost impossible to find an all-encompassing definition. Groups have gathered to discuss this very issue, both seriously and with ale-fed humour, both by studying the old Irish Brehon Laws and by studying their navels. But there is simply no sacred scripture which all Druids can refer to. There is no one god, or even one pantheon, which all Druids revere as the divine guiding force. There are no prophets who have laid down great truths together with ritual obligations – just mixtures of historical and mythical heroes.

In many ways, Druidry is even more complex than Paganism or another broad spirituality such as Hinduism. It is a truly polytheistic faith, within which can be found space and honour for any deity or any concept of deity, together with their priests, devotees and philosophers. There are many within the tradition who call themselves Christian, while some assert that Druidry is not a religion at all, not even necessarily a spirituality, but simply a philosophy of living.

The majority of Druids, however, are in one way or another Pagan. In making that statement, though, it is necessary to clarify Paganism as it is most widely used within the tradition.

The notion that a Pagan is anyone who does not subscribe to one of the three monotheistic Middle Eastern religions of Christianity, Judaism and Islam is now disregarded, even though it is still found in many dictionaries. The idea that a Pagan is a rural (as opposed to an urban) dweller is closer, but still a little narrow and misleading. The more accurate definition is that a Pagan is someone who reveres the spirits and deities of his local environment – of the earth beneath his feet, of his spring or source of water, his woodlands and rivers, his fields and buildings, his sun and moon and rain, and more; of everything that makes up the world that exists immediately around him.

The majority of Druids, whoever their gods may be, would accept that this is a key aspect of their practice. While some might worship the spirit of a spring, for example, as a deity, one of many gods, and others would understand the spirit to be an aspect of a higher god or creative force, any practising Druid would be sure to make offerings and prayers of thanks each time they visited that sacred place.

## AN EARTH-ANCESTOR SPIRITUALITY

It is also possible to describe Druidry as an Earth-ancestor spirituality. Even if we accept ideas that Druidry was brought to Britain by ancient Egyptians whose knowledge was given them by refugee Atlanteans, which to many seems rather a wild soul dream, the essence of the faith is still the honouring of the fertile Earth and the father/mother bringers of life and wisdom.

The more widely accepted possible origins of the faith take us back into the primitive cultures of neolithic Europe and to the motivating drive behind any religion: the need to understand

the world around us in our search for survival, together with some way of assuring the future through the fertility of the land and tribe. In this, Druidry connects with all the other Earth-ancestor traditions around the globe, such as the Native American, the Maori and Huna, the Aboriginal, the Romany and the indigenous spiritualities of Africa and Asia.

Science may have given us answers to many of our forebears' questions and crises, but honouring the mysteries and manifestations of life is still a profoundly sacred and rewarding act, and it lies deep within the heart of modern Druidry.

## GOOD BOOTS AND A COMPASS

Understanding Druidry in this way clarifies the honouring of the ancestors and honouring of the land as the two fundamental points of the tradition.

The ancestors begin with our parents and go as far back as we can imagine. Many of us know little or nothing of our forebears, our lineage blurring beyond our grandparents and disappearing into mud with the turn of the last century, but to the Druid this is not a constraint. The ancestors exist as a people in spirit and include not only our bloodline, but also those who lived and died on the land beneath us, however long or short a time we ourselves (or our bloodline) have been living there too. Our spiritual ancestry is also honoured, that is, all those who have practised within the spiritual tradition, our teachers and guides, both living and dead.

Furthermore, there are Druids whose blood is not of these islands, whose ancestors worshipped different gods in different lands and different climates, and it is understood that this must influence the practice of those Druids.

The gods of our ancestors are also honoured, as they too are a part of what has made us who we are.

As within Druidry there is a general acceptance of the transmigration of souls, without limitation to one bloodline or indeed one species, the act of giving to the ancestors is done with a conscious understanding that in doing so the Druid is also giving to, and honouring, the spirits of his descendants, through his blood, the Earth and the tradition.

The practice of the faith is also affected by the immediate environment, for Druids will respond to the Earth around them, listening to its needs and the songs and stories of the spirits within it. So, a Druid born and brought up on the Lancashire moors will have a different practice from one who was born in the heat of Florida and now lives in Kent, or, indeed, a Druid from north Wales who now lives in Japan.

The way in which Druids consider the Earth sacred varies according their concept of deity. Most Druids are animists, understanding that all aspects of nature are vibrant with spirit, yet while many Druids acknowledge some spirits to be divine or embodied by a deity, such as river spirits, the moon, a forest and so on, others understand them simply to be a creative expression or an aspect of a higher god or goddess. All Druids honour the Earth, though for many their work is confined to their spiritual practice and their locality, while others are involved in global environmentalism.

Two effects, which in themselves are an important part of defining Druidry, emerge from the practice of honouring the ancestors and the land. The Druid will accept without reservation another person's individual experience, their perspective, their gods and their spiritual practice (so long as this does not dishonour the Earth or the ancestors): perfect tolerance. And the Druid relates to every creature, of rock or wood or leaf, the finned and feathered folk, the winged ones and the four legged, the crawlers and slitherers, the hairy, furry and smooth-skinned ones, as well

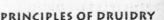

as human folk, primarily as spirit and therefore with an equal right to life, respect and dignity: perfect equality.

*Understanding these elements, the land and the ancestors, as two powerful basics of modern Druidry, perhaps we can stop for a moment. Think about them. How much do you honour your parents? What do you know of your blood ancestors and of the ancestors of the Earth beneath your feet? In what way do you or could you honour them, acknowledging their spirit, their experience, their gifts? And what of the teachers who have been your guides, with lessons that were hard as well as those where you succeeded?*

*What too of your attitude towards the Earth? Think about how you have received from the Earth and in what way you have given thanks for that, in what way you have consciously reciprocated, giving back.*

*Then slide those basics on, as if they were sturdy walking boots, and tie the laces well. As you travel into the tradition, they will give you sure footing. And looking up at the road ahead, take as a compass the tenets of tolerance and equality. They will bring you back to the path, should doubt cloud your way.*

## THE JOURNEY

My first suggestion was to stop reading, to get out and walk the land, leaving behind our civilized world to find the world of nature where the vibrations of humanity are not omnipresent, wild spaces where, no longer distracted by the threat of others' judgement, or by our inhibitions and the things we feel we ought to do, we can better feel ourselves, beneath the masks and the roles we play, spaces where we are strong enough to consider how we can change and flow.

In your wilderness you gave an offering of yourself, both to the Earth in thanks and to those Druids who are the ancestors and guardians of the tradition, expressing your desire and commitment to discover more. Such offerings blend our celebration of who we are and what we have been given with our willingness to sacrifice something of ourselves, a part of our strength and abundance, and they help us to see more clearly both what we have and how we are willing to change.

It is in the arms of nature, in the colours of the sunset, in the dragonflies' dance, in the thoughts that glide through us as we watch the horizon through the grass, feeling the Earth beneath our body, listening, awake, that the spirit of Druidry glows. The Earth itself, with the tides and cycles of nature, is the holy scripture of the tradition and the source of our understanding of it. These words are no more than a rough map and field guide, with suggestions and ideas about what might be seen along the way.

There is no need to struggle to believe in anything, nor to love and follow blindly. Druidry is a spiritual journey of the individual's soul, one that honours each unique vision and expression. It inspires ideas which are understood to be simply ideas, until experience transforms them into knowing.

## WHO MIGHT WE MEET ALONG THE WAY?

Any path into Druidry will at some stage lead the traveller to encounter other Druids and seekers. Treading the path alone is often a necessary stage of the journey, but to join others can be both rewarding and instructive.

While those the traveller might meet may come from any part of the spectrum of Druidic expression, they may also be working on very different levels within the tradition. The mystical spirituality at the core of Druidry is a place of profound personal dedication which inspires the Druid to focus his whole life into his faith. Around the core exists the wider community of Druidry where the intensity and discipline are not so demanding. This outer body has emerged over the past ten years with the huge growth in interest in Druidry and the

greater accessibility offered by open and public ceremonies. This has allowed many to get involved who would not be ready for or interested in the mystical journey, preferring to leave that to a priesthood, yet who want to learn a little more, to gather together to celebrate the festivals and rites, and strive to live by Druidic principles.

Some of the Druids we may meet along the way, however, are not a part of the new and growing body of modern Druidry. They are guides and teachers that we reach through the subtle senses of our minds. They exist in the inner worlds, through the mists. The offering you gave at the beginning of your journey, if sincerely given, will have inspired such a teacher to take an interest in you and your path of discovery, on whatever level of curiosity or commitment you choose to travel. If you are willing to be open, of heart and mind, to listen and to hear, to see a different world through a Druidic perspective, that guide will remain with you. You may be aware of them – either already or in a time to come.

Whoever we meet, it is worth remembering that any individual, in body or in spirit, does not represent any other part of the tradition or the community other than themselves.

## WHERE DOES THE PATH GO?

Druidry is a sacred journey of discovering the beauty and sanctity of all life, both physical and spiritual. Yet it is not enough for the Druid simply to know that all creation is sacred: the path leads beyond that point to a place where they can reach into that divine reality. The journey of the Druid is to feel the touch of the gods, in whatever way they perceive them, by reaching – as body and spirit – into the spirit that vitalizes the world.

One of the keys of the tradition is the *awen*. This is an old Welsh word which can be translated as 'flowing spirit' and is understood to mean the flow of divine inspiration which comes at that point of exquisite contact, pouring out from a deity and into a Druid. With the inspiration comes the energy, the empowerment needed for the Druid to allow that sacred inspiration to pour through them into creativity. The endless task of the Druid is to perfect this process.

The nature of the creativity inspired by this blissful connection with the divine can come in many forms, according to the skills of the individual, his own needs or those of the person or people for or with whom he is working. Poetry and music, the telling of stories and magical myths are the most commonly associated works of creative expression that emerge out of Druidry. Others' inspiration comes through art, healing, teaching, divination, gardening, politics and indeed any aspect of modern life where there is the potential for freeing the soul's true and full creativity.

# WHERE DOES
# IT COME FROM?

L et us begin our journey by stopping, as we step onto the path, and looking out over the landscape from which that path emerged.

## THE WINDING PATH

It is not possible to see the path as one unbroken track all the way back to the distant horizon. We might believe or sense that the path of the tradition is not broken, but its course is not consistently clear. There are Druid groups which have records which are said to carry their own threads of the tradition back to the very beginning of time, but generally it is understood that these are not factual histories so much as stories that guide the student deeper into the mystical experience of her faith. So the path that we see bends out of view, emerging elsewhere before disappearing once again. At some points there appear to be two or three distinct tracks, then none at all.

For those entering an old tradition with great enthusiasm reined to the belief that there is a strong and continuous line from ancient Druidry to the present day, being faced with this broken path can be disenchanting. Yet Druidry exists as a growing tradition. How can this be so?

*Looking over the track, consider how important the issue of continuity is to you. Does it feel necessary for your commitment to the journey to know that the tradition has a documented history? Why?*

## THE SOURCES

For some modern Druids, searching for sources of the tradition is an important part of their spiritual adventure. Yet as more information spills out – from both academia and the Earth herself – the facts become less clear. The romantic veils which were spread over the uncertainties during the last 200–300 years have been slipping off, revealing the gaps in sharp focus.

From prehistory there is virtually no evidence that might allow us to piece together the spiritual practices of these islands. Despite the wealth of New Stone Age and Bronze Age sites scattered over the land, there is nothing from that period that gives any true clarity in terms of deities revered or ceremonies performed.

With the spread of Iron Age culture across Europe we find a little more, though in comparison with the Continent there is still almost nothing to go on in the British Isles. It is not until the Romans first arrived in the middle of the first century BCE that a clearer picture emerges about the religions of these lands. Yet as Druidry has long been connected with Celtic culture, Classical sources tend to have been overlooked in favour of medieval Irish and Welsh literature. For some Druids, the work of eighteenth and nineteenth-century scholars, itself built on many different roots, is sufficient as a source for modern practice. In the same way, there are many today whose understanding of Druidry is sourced in the work of modern writers and researchers who have created a tradition in their own style.

Yet Druidry is not necessarily based on any of these sources. As a spirituality deeply rooted in the land, it has evolved through the needs of the land and the people who have relied upon that land, shifting, adapting, balancing just as our environment does. The Druidry of 420 BCE, when the iron-working culture was spreading into Britain, would no doubt have been very different from that of 580 CE, when the first poems were being written by the Bard Taliesin and the tribal battles were fierce between the Saxons and the British. Another 1,200 years on and the land, the culture, is very different again, with the rise of a romantic Celtic identity and the Industrial Revolution at 'full steam ahead'. Viewing the landscape and various stretches of track in search of the nature of the tradition, what appears most important is not the continuity but the colours, the detail and images that catch our eye.

## THE EARLIEST TRACES

The earliest images date back to a time when the climate of Britain became gradually warmer and the period which we call the neolithic began. This provided the first evidence of a spiritual practice. The neolithic long barrows, chambered passage graves dating as far back as 4400 BCE, are now thought to be the oldest human-made monuments on Earth. Though thousands still exist across western Europe, each one differs sufficiently to blur any attempts to focus on a pattern. Each was used over many hundreds of years, with the cleaned bones of the dead being placed in the tomb, but as to the rites that accompanied the task we have few clues. The bodies, men, women and children of all ages, were excarnated in half a dozen different ways, even those placed in the same barrow, from the use of fire to carrion birds. The area in front of the entrance to the barrows

was a place of ritual, but what was done and by whom we can only search for within our soul memories.

Whoever the priests were, the elements they were dealing with would have seemed powerful indeed. The energy of these graves is rich, dark, earthy, born out of a time with few certainties when the world was vast, and nature wild and hungry. We can imagine more: that language was rough, sicknesses fatal and deeply feared, the air thick with smells and alive with colour, our bodies critically dependent on instinct for survival. Any measure of understanding about the mysteries of the stars, the seasons and tides, the patterns of growth, the movements of the wild herds, about birth and death, would have been deeply honoured. Those who held the knowledge, however sketchy or superstitious, would have been revered – and feared.

*Take some time and go to an ancient long barrow. If there are none accessible, take yourself there in your imagination. Either way, be sure to take with you an offering for the spirits, for the ancestors, their gods and the guardians of the site. Remember that offerings should be quickly biodegradable or edible for local wildlife; ideally there should be no trace left after just a few days.*

*Before you approach the grave, sit quietly and relax, calming yourself to a point where you will be able to listen. Then, quietly and with respect, walk up to the barrow. Walk around it, down its length, staying relaxed, listening. Spend time in the area before the entrance and allow your mind to drift, envisioning what might have happened there. What would the role of the priest have been? If the barrow is open, when you are ready and if you wish, enter the passageway. What do you feel?*

*Leave your offerings, in peace and with thanks. As you leave the site, do so consciously, disconnecting from its energy with respect.*

The weather continued to grow warmer. Over the next 1,500 years, our ancestors began to develop an understanding of

agriculture, felling trees to make fields, working with different crops. With the stability of farming, the population began to increase and spread. By 3200 BCE the climate was almost Mediterranean. Yet around that time, something shifted, and there followed about 200 years of tremendous upheaval which seems to have been caused by violent intertribal conflict.

The circular bank and ditch earthworks which were once considered to be later Iron Age hill forts are now thought to have been constructed during this time of instability. The old long barrows across most of the island were carefully blocked up, using massive and unmovable stones, perhaps to seal in the power of the old ancestral spirits, perhaps to ensure they were not disturbed, perhaps through fear. In Ireland and the north-west reaches of Britain, some of the old barrows were built upon with new tombs, creating developed passage graves such as Newgrange, implying that here there was a different attitude towards the older religion.

Around 3000 BCE stability returned, yet things were changed. After a millennium and a half of the oval or rectangular barrow the focus had altered, taking us into the era of the circle. Bank and ditch structures became common, many developing into circles of wooden poles and, later, stones. Some of these have survived or been recreated, such as the huge Avebury ring in Wiltshire or the smaller, darker circle of the Rollrights in Oxfordshire. Throughout this time, too, round barrows were built, each the tomb of one person, no doubt a prominent figure in the social structure, the bones being buried and the barrow closed, not to be reused.

The priests of these people would have had a very different task from those of the earlier neolithic period. The energy or atmosphere of these sites is lighter, more open; the weather was warm and nurturing. It was a period of growth and change, with new pressures arising within a growing population.

Some of these may have been expressed in the building of Stonehenge, probably the most astounding accomplishment of the period. While the open circles seem to have been made to hold many hundreds of people, with all who gathered, perhaps from far and wide, having a chance to watch the proceedings, it was quite different at Stonehenge. Here the rituals would have been difficult if not impossible to observe in detail from anywhere but within the confines of the small inner circle. The final stages were completed around 2000 BCE, obviously by a ruling élite which effectively wiped out religious practice at all the other main sites throughout a significant stretch of the country.

*Take yourself to an ancient circle, in body if you are within reach, or within your imagination. Either way, remember to take appropriate offerings. It may be a stone circle, or a bank and ditch earthwork, or perhaps a place where a circle of wood or stones used to stand but where now only a faint impression remains in the landscape.*

*Once there, relax, letting go as you sit by a tree, lie in the grass or just meander, feeling the touch of the earth beneath your feet. Allow impressions of the place to seep into your senses.*

*What do you think caused the period of disturbance? What would have been the role of the priest during the 1,500 years of the circle era? What were the needs of the people? What of the needs of the land?*

*Present your offerings, in peace and with thanks, before you leave, disconnecting from the site with respect.*

The arrival of bronze appears to have made no major impact on the spiritual practices of the islands, nor indeed did the coming of iron. It was before the iron-working culture found its way to Britain that another change occurred and the circles were abandoned around 1200 BCE. The cause of this appears to have been the weather.

The temperature had suddenly begun to fall, reaching its lowest point around 1000 BCE. The clear skies and starry nights which so beautifully attuned with the stone temples built out on the moors and meadows were a thing of the past. It rained. The temperature plunged to around that of what is now southern Sweden – and with no clear predictability in the weather, any solar, lunar or stellar alignments in a temple or tomb became a virtual irrelevance.

The cause of this climate change is debatable. Volcanic activity in Iceland may have added to the problem, but perhaps more interesting for us nowadays is the issue of just how much the first farmers had cleared the forests that had previously covered the land. Certainly we know that huge tracts of deforested land were reclaimed by nature, becoming bog, which, to the Iron Age farmer, was not only useless but also dangerous.

The spiritual focus shifted from the point within the circle where the brilliant sky touched the Earth to the new elemental force which was driving through the lives of the people: water. Archaeological evidence now reveals for us the wealth of metalwork, jewellery and weaponry that was offered into rivers, lakes and wells at this time, as the people called out to the spirits of the water.

What of the priests of these people?

*After the dark era of the tombs, then the warmth of the circle era, we come to the era of water.*

*This time take a walk to the nearest or most powerful source of fresh water to your home, and there allow yourself to understand its energy, its power and presence. Feel something of all that it gives you. Throw your offerings into the water with thanks and respect.*

# WHO WERE THE CELTS?

It is often declared that Druids were the priesthood of the Celtic people. If this was so, where are the Celts in the changing colours and climate of these islands?

The term *Keltoi* was first used by Greek historians writing in the fifth century BCE to refer to some of the peoples living north of the Alps. It was this reference that archaeologists of the last century recalled when uncovering evidence of a tribal culture in early Iron Age Austria. The finds, from almost a thousand graves, were dated to around 800 BCE, and were the oldest iron artefacts, tools and weaponry to emerge out of the Bronze Age culture that existed across Europe. This iron-working culture also appeared to be the first extensively to use horses in warfare. Bronze objects and pictures inscribed on pottery of the era give us an impression of the lifestyle, with representations of what could be seen to be musicians, Bards, dancers, priest figures and deities.

The culture spread, no doubt in part because of the natural movement of peoples who were strengthened by their skills both in battle and in agriculture, but also through trading and the dissemination of those skills. The first traces are found in southern Britain from the early sixth century BCE and thereafter it appeared to move slowly south-west to the Iberian peninsula, eastwards to Turkey and north to Scotland and Ireland. When Julius Caesar referred to the *Celtae*, 400 years after the Greeks, he was describing a people of central and southern France. It's difficult then to be distinct about who the Celts were. Celtic culture is simply that of the Iron Age people of Europe.

When that culture began to find its way over to Britain, the focus of spiritual practice was on the water spirits that were holding onto the weather reins and soaking the Earth.

# THE CLASSICAL SOURCES

For many modern Druids it is the ancient tombs and circles, together with nature's forests and rivers, mountains and meadows, that are the focus of their spirituality, giving them a doorway into the mysteries. Anything human-made after the time of the Roman invasion is seldom held to be sacred in its own right, for now the people themselves appear and a bridge is made through a human connection. Perhaps this is due to the change in the clues – from now on it is the people who supply them.

The writings of Roman warriors and historians give us the first evidence (if politically biased) of the ancient religions. The picture they paint is of Druids being an educated élite in the society the Romans encountered, influential in political and legal affairs, in philosophy, history and learning, healing and magic, as well as overseeing or carrying out religious ceremonial.

Some writers, such as Tacitus and Strabo, writing at a time when Gaul was under Roman rule and Britain almost defeated, emphasized the barbaric nature of the culture, its laws and religion. With an almost missionary zeal they urge that the tribes be 'civilized' into a Roman sense of order and principle, and abhor the apparent use of human sacrifice (though it might be noted that at the same time this was said to be happening in Gaul the bloodthirsty games in the Circus at Rome were still in full swing). Other writers, however, such as the Greek Hippolytus, were more concerned with the Druids' philosophy and learning, which seemed to them honourable beyond the decadent degeneracy of their own culture.

## THE WORD 'DRUID'

Julius Caesar was one of the first to write of Druids, in the first century BCE, and was one of the few who actually knew a Druid: the tribal chief Divitiacus. It is through Caesar's work that we first find the Gallic word 'Druid', implying that they were not simply priests, but also held significant political power. The origins of the word itself, however, are debated.

It is generally thought that the first part comes from the word for 'oak', which in many European languages is close to *drui*: *drus* in Greek, *daur* in Irish, *derw* in Welsh (where the word for Druid is *derwydd*). The latter part may come from the Indo-European root word *wid*, meaning 'wisdom'. The Druid then is suggested to be the one who holds the wisdom of the oak.

## AN ORAL TRADITION

One of the clues we are given by Caesar is that the centre for Druid training, at the time of his writing, was Britain, where it was understood the philosophy and the religious practice had originated.

Yet this provokes more questions, for if Druidry emerged from Britain and the Celtic culture came from eastern central Europe, was Druidry the spirituality of Britain before the Celts arrived? Were the priests known by a different name, though their ideology was still the source of later Druidry? Did the practice develop out of the merging of the Celtic culture and the land of Britain?

For many Druids these questions are, however, irrelevant: Druidry is a spirituality of the land and the people, both of which change, evolve, adapt. Many believe that the faith was inspired by the landscape, the climate, the tribes and their ancestors of Britain. Yet there was never a beginning point, only a gradual evolution.

We do know that the Druids never wrote down any aspect of their religion. One reason for this was, no doubt, to reduce the risk of their teachings being desecrated and misused, but also, as an oral tradition, it held in highest esteem the power of the mind and of memory, yet never risked the fate of being tied down to one scripture or set of prophecies. It remained alive, evading containment, moulding itself around each new influence that proved worthy.

*Many are drawn to Druidry through a deep inner connection with the word 'Celtic' or 'Keltic'. They may have a blood link to Gaelic Ireland or Scotland, or to the old British people of Wales or Cornwall. What is your connection?*

*Find an hour or two of quiet and sit down with a piece of paper. In the middle write the word 'Celtic', allowing your creativity to flow, decorating the word until it becomes a focal image. Use colours if it helps you to express all that you want to. From that central word, allow your mind to flow freely, writing down words in a web of connecting associations.*

*What does the page reveal to you?*

## THE ROMANS' CONTRIBUTION

The Romans did attempt to eradicate the Druids, yet it was not their religion which threatened the polytheistic and Pagan Roman imperialists, but the political power which they held over the tribes. Many ideas and assumptions have been offered about this issue, with various emotional and intellectual investments weighting the arguments, but we have no clear historical facts.

We do know, however, that the Druids' influence was significant, over leaders and kings, trade routes and disputes, and attitudes towards the incoming peoples. The Romans didn't come for the purpose of settling, though, they came to take control, and everything of value to each British kingdom, their natural and human resources, trade links and knowledge, was overseen by the Druids. It isn't surprising, then, that the Druids were often at the heart of insurrections against the conquering armies.

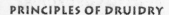

As the Roman forces moved across Britain, the influence of the Druids diminished. Their role was never quite the same again, although in Ireland and the farthest reaches of Scotland, which the Romans never reached as a conquering army, their work did continue. In Ireland, there is mention of a Druid still working as advisor to the King of Cashel as late as the tenth century, but by then the next force of Rome had swept through: Christianity.

The Roman invasion wasn't objected to across the board. After all, it was a strong culture, rich with learning, literature, art and technical advances. There were many tribal kings and, indeed, Druids who welcomed it. Over the 400 years that Rome ruled in these islands, a blended Romano-British culture evolved, which before the coming of Christianity was a wonderful Pagan mixture.

In terms of sources for modern Druids to understand their spiritual ancestry, the Romans did not only leave their writings, but also pictures and inscriptions about the nature of the gods. As good Pagans, the pre-Christian Romans who arrived on these shores automatically looked to the spirits and deities of the land to guide and help them as they walked upon its soil: without the protection, the nourishment, the acceptance of the land, the Romans knew they would not be able to survive.

There are many examples of Roman-built temples which are simply a development of a previous Celtic shrine. There are examples too of Romans who honoured on their altars the spirits of the land whom they considered to be the local deities, as well as the god or gods brought with them from their homeland. It is through these inscriptions that modern Druids are discovering the names of the old gods.

*Spend some time considering the influence of the Romans, as you did the Celts.*

*Find out where your nearest Romano-British site is. Your local library will help. If possible, go there. Spend some time freely wandering, relaxing, listening. What do you feel, what do you envision? Remember to take an appropriate offering to leave as a gift of respect and thanks, and to disconnect fully and consciously whenever you leave an old or sacred site.*

*If you cannot find or visit a site near you, arrange a trip to a well known site, such as the Roman baths in the Somerset town of Bath, sacred to the British goddess Sulis and the Roman goddess Minerva.*

When the empire was under attack from barbarians in the mid-fifth century, the Roman withdrawal from Britain was only in effect a removal of the military and governing bodies. Those who had come with the empire and had settled in Britain remained in what was now a richly multi-cultural land, the diversity of influences having been nurtured by the free movement of people and trade throughout the Roman world. It was a land, though, which by the fifth century had a strong ruling class who were mainly Christian.

That mix of influences made its mark on the native religion of the islands, but when the Roman armies left it wasn't long before new invaders were landing on the eastern shores, beginning with the Saxons and followed by the Viking Danes, both of whom arrived as Pagans into a Britain ruled by mainly Christian kings.

## THE MEDIEVAL TALES

With the Druids' influence diminished under Roman rule, then the tyranny of the new Christianity, the essence of the faith survived most strongly through the art and craft of the Bards. The first written source for the Druid tradition from a non-Classical origin dates from the late sixth century onwards: the medieval Bardic literature of Wales and Ireland.

Bards were a part of the Druid caste and, though clues are sparse, it is thought that the process of becoming a Druid involved many years in Bardic training, learning the histories and ancestry of the people the Druids served. The role of the Bards was to affirm the identity of the tribe and the strength of the king, often with genealogies that reached back to the gods. With tireless eulogies the Bards praised the courage of the warriors and the beauty of the women, entertaining and richly painting the virtues of those who supported them.

The Bards were deemed no threat to the Roman invaders, and they continued as entertainers and storytellers, now not only keeping the wisdom of their craft but also carrying much of the Druid wisdom, wrapped in a different cloth. Where their colleges were not changed into something unrecognizable by Roman or Christian development, they continued with the old teachings. Indeed, it wasn't until the seventeenth century that the last Bardic college was closed in Ireland and not until the early eighteenth century in Scotland.

By the sixth century the Saxons were moving west in search of land on which to settle, and those who could not or would not tolerate the change were being driven west before them, into Wales and southern Scotland. This evoked two strands of interest in the people who were under this pressure: first, from those incomers who were curious about the culture which their presence was diluting, if not destroying; and second, from within these people themselves who felt a rising need to preserve that culture.

Who were these people? They were the Romano-British with, at the fringes, the tribal British who had been slightly less affected by 400 years of Roman civilization. As for their culture, by now the British language had taken on a good deal of the Roman Latin, in structure, sound and vocabulary, on top of the Celtic influences which had spread across Europe prior to that.

With the new invasions, it was now encountering the language of Germanic Saxons, and it was around this time, as an assertion of British identity, that the language which we now call Middle Welsh was created. It was an extremely complex language which perhaps was never meant to be freely spoken, but was devised by the Bards as a language of poetry to be chanted or sung, and as a medium for retaining an ancestral culture which was under threat.

In Scotland, the Pictish people had been driven north by invading Irish around 300 CE and the Irish Gaelic language and culture became dominant, effectively wiping out that of the earlier Picts.

So the majority of early Irish and Welsh literature developed not as a natural progression from oral tradition into literacy, but as an assertive expression of cultural identity.

Some historians would claim that the tradition which these books so beautifully express had already died and the writers were reaching back through a gap of some few hundred years into a culture about which they had little understanding. Certainly, the stories, poetry and songs are not a pure rendition of the old tales. They are written with a distinct if beautifully creative overlay of both Graeco-Roman influences and the Christianity which was the active faith of the majority of the writers. The latter not only slid in by being merely the mentality of the writer, but also as a conscious censoring hand, changing the focus and reworking the tales to include their own god(s).

For many modern Druids, these tales are of exquisite value as sources of their own spiritual inspiration and are not diminished in value because of the mix of cultures. They are another expression of the evolution of a spirituality which honours creativity and the gods of all creation.

So the historical sources of Druidry are not entirely clear. The track is winding and appears from a distance rather haphazard. Yet for those who stand upon it, who feel the Earth, its pebbles and grass beneath their feet, it is a blaze of wild colours.

As a religion of these islands, of their flora and fauna, and the power of the gifts that every spirit has brought to their shores, the deep wisdom of their priests, the tradition offers the person who stands looking back for inspiration thousands of places to dive into and breathe deeply. And if we understand Druidry to be a spirituality whose focus is the search for divine and perfect inspiration, inspiration that gives us a profound knowing and freedom, a true creativity, we must also accept that each soul will find that source in her own way.

# THE SPECTRUM OF DRUIDRY

The majority of those who study and work within the faith do so with an acceptance of its drifting origins and evolution, in a land which has been washed by so many cultural tides. The uncertainty is smoothed by the understanding that Druidry has always continued, evolving through the millennia, existing on the inner planes of the human collective psyche and in the worlds of spirit beyond the mist.

Though many in the tradition study within a recognized structure, there is a strong belief that our deepest teaching comes directly from those inner worlds. In the process of becoming a Druid, we learn to access our teachers in spirit, those who hold the ageless wisdom together with the stories of our people, the land and our heritage.

It is not surprising then that within modern Druidry there is such a wide spectrum of belief and practice. For the newcomer to the faith, any personal inkling about what Druidry is might be entirely thwarted by encountering one Druid and warmly affirmed in meeting another.

With the understanding that each individual, with his own sources of inspiration, his own archetype of 'Druid', his own inner teachers and guides, will hold an independent view of the faith, it is a difficult task to divide the spectrum into larger groups. Yet the desire to find others who share similar perspectives, with its potential for spiritual kinship and the intimacy of common experience, does bring people together.

By looking at these shared perspectives we can define some distinct groups, though it must be understood that individuals are likely to meander across any boundaries I may suggest.

## THE STRENGTH OF THE CELTIC

Though the Iron Age Celtic peoples may be the first culture of these lands that left enough evidence for us to grasp any idea of their ways of life, it is the medieval Irish and Welsh texts that have had the most direct influence on wide areas of modern Druidry.

To understand these stories and poems we must go to the texts themselves. Nowadays there is a good range in various translations. Another useful guide is to look back at the way in which the Bardic tradition may have developed.

As a part of the Druid caste the Bards were supported by their communities. While the Druid held the power, performing ceremonies and rites as judge and magician, the role of the Bard was quite different. It was his task to know by heart the histories of the people and the land, and to recite these for the tribal king or chief, or any who would pay according to his skill and status. He would remind the community of oaths made, commitments declared, battles won, triumphant quests. He would affirm through stories the connection of the tribe with the sacred nature of its land, its mountains and springs, tombs, rivers and mounds, the animals and earth spirits, and, most importantly perhaps, the tribe's connection with the gods, through genealogies which took the bloodline of the king back to the old gods themselves. The Bard was the force that gave the people their identity.

When the influence of the Druids was diminishing under repression, some of their old wisdom was robed in the Bardic tradition, held in the stories, the myths of the people and their land.

For some modern Druids these tales are a source of profound guidance and spiritual inspiration. In many ways they act as a link between this eve of the twenty-first century and the pre-Christian Druids. They are rich with intriguing clues. In the Irish stories in particular, there are many tales of Druids, though whether these are drawn from an authentic memory of Druidry or are an expression of a medieval fantasy of Druids we cannot tell. The Graeco-Roman influence is certainly underlying, the Christianity often an obvious overlay. The earliest surviving Irish manuscripts are from the twelfth century, though these contain clues that the stories were written a few hundred years before.

The earlier Welsh poems, rather than the stories, contain references to Druids, though in a vaguer, less specific way than the Irish, as if alluding to an older, more distant memory. Here the Bards who tell the tales are working on what feels more like a romantic reconstruction.

*Find and read some of the old Irish and Welsh stories (suggestions can be found in Chapter Nine), getting a feel for both cultures and the differences and similarities between them. If the opportunity arises, hear a modern Bard telling the stories, perhaps in a traditional way, accompanied by a harp. Do they awake some part of your soul with a deep familiarity? Does the Irish feel more comfortable or the Welsh?*

*Choose one story and read it again and again. What does this story say to you, what does it teach you? How? Recite it aloud. Take it to a place that seems appropriate to the story, perhaps by a river, a hazel tree, a well, and tell it again there. Allow it to slip into your memory. How does it feel to hold it now inside you?*

There is an element within modern Druidry which craves this sense of Celtic identity. In the search for self, for belonging, for roots, there are many who seek the Celtic and do so in the most part through the medieval literature. Finding inner strength through a personal connection with an ancient heritage can be an important part of the journey, offering that intimacy of shared experience and community of spirit which is felt to be deeply rooted, whether the individual has a blood link to a modern Celtic land or merely a soul allegiance.

The nature of the texts offer a great deal of scope. The images in the stories and poems can be interpreted in many ways and, if taken together with snatches of art, inscriptions, temples and the ancient monuments, offer the seeker a wealth of information from which each soul can find inspiration, beauty, strength, social equality and tribal cohesion – whatever we are searching for as individuals – to regain and re-inject into our world.

There are areas of modern Druidry where the process is an active assertion to protect the Celtic identity, and energy is invested in reinvigorating the Welsh, Cornish and Gaelic languages, their folklore and traditions, their old magical arts and medicines, the stories and poems of the old tribes and their lands, as an assertion against the spread of what is seen to be the monochrome global culture of the English/American.

There are also those within the faith for whom the journey is an intellectual quest to discover the authentic nature of Druidry. These Druids mainly reject any work later than the medieval texts, which they use very specifically, extracting what is useful and relevant to our era and creating a modern Druidry which is deemed to have an authentic ancient base. Needless to say, a great deal of the darker side, the elements of sorcery and sacrifice particularly evident in the Irish stories, is left behind.

A greater proportion of those within the Druid tradition relate to the Celtic literature as works of creativity, not potential sources of authenticity, content that modern Druidry needs no validation from the past, having evolved naturally into its present state, always existing on the inner planes.

There is an understanding that the Celtic soul dwells within all who live in lands where the Celts settled, and is not restricted to the farthest reaches of Europe's western seaboard which the Romans, Christians, Jutes and Danes, Angles and Saxons barely touched. It also dwells within all who have blood and soul connections to these lands, though they may live elsewhere. With the understanding that Celtic was a culture and not a race, the majority of Druids find no valid base for exclusivity.

Within the medieval texts, together with all that is understood to be of the ancient Celts, are found qualities that inspire: courage and equality, creativity and respect, the profound connection to the Earth and to the tribal ancestors. It is through the search for these qualities that many modern Druids walk a path that leads them to the spirit of the Celtic people, or what is felt to be the embodiment of all that is Celtic, and that is the Celtic deities.

Not all Druids hold Celtic gods as their principal deities and not all Pagans who revere Celtic gods are Druids. Wiccans, traditional Witches and those who follow shamanic paths may all work with Celtic gods, vitalizing their connections to the land and their ancestry. What makes them other than Druids may simply be their archetypes, definitions and guides – or their tradition, energy and practice may be very different indeed.

Yet even among those Druids who do not hold Celtic gods as their main deities, the Celtic is widely acknowledged and honoured as a key influence in the evolution of these lands and the development of the faith.

# THE CHRISTIAN ANGLE

A significant proportion of Druids do not identify themselves as primarily Pagan. There are those who declare Druidry is not a spirituality or religion, and many hold that it is a path of mysticism, a wisdom school, within which one can hold any religious belief. This allows for Druids who are purely searching through the mind, without an acknowledgement of spirit other than as life force energy. A good number of these non-Pagans blend the philosophies of Druidry with those of Christianity.

For a Druid Christian, the Earth and all creation is an expression of the deity as presence, and therefore deeply sacred. While there are Christians who acknowledge this without moving into Druidry, others find that the philosophy significantly strengthens and broaden their faith. Deepening the acceptance, within the framework of Christianity, of the power and beauty of the divine gift of the physical, there is opened up also the respect for sexuality, for birth, our genetic inheritance and with it reverence for our ancestors. The Earth, its flora and fauna, humanity and all creation become an altar to God. In an age when environmentalism, the importance of family and community, interest in folk traditions and natural medicine are all increasing, the point at which Druidry and Christianity meet becomes clearer.

The openness of Druidic language, which allows for any colour and mixture of god and ceremony within its essential philosophy, invites the Christian to relate his own imagery into Druidry. There are many points of meeting; for instance, the Mabon, the sacred child, the sun reborn in the darkness of Midwinter, is comfortably woven with the birth of Jesus. The importance of divine sacrifice is also shared, acknowledged in Druidry at the harvest with the death of the corn god, the cycle

38     of decay and regeneration through the seasons of the year, and the process of dying to the self in the mystical journey to inner peace.

Christians within Druidry come from many different churches, from the simplicity of Quakerism to the highly ritualistic, from the focus on Jesus to the honouring of a thousand saints, and each interacts with the Druid philosophy in a different way, each creating a different Druidic practice. Some strands of Christianity are easily plaited with Druidry, such as those where particular saints act as spirit guardians at, for example, healing springs.

There are some Druid Orders who only accept Christians into their membership, while others would not accept non-Pagans. The vast majority, however, are not restrictive in this way and, indeed, many Druids actively work on the borders where the two traditions meet, bridging the gaps and addressing issues where misunderstandings have arisen. Interfaith conferences held over the last five years have inspired an increasing tolerance and understanding, not only at the border points but also more deeply within each tradition.

A number of those who blend the two do so from a point outside the Christian Church, although remaining within its faith. These Christian or Christic Druids retain a clear understanding of Christian deity, honouring Jesus Christ as the saviour, the key and the gateway in whichever way they are most accustomed to or inspired by, yet stepping away from the structure of the religion which they regard as political.

For the wider Pagan and polytheistic Druid community, these Christic Druids are acknowledged and respected simply as revering another of the numerous gods.

Some Christians within Druidry describe themselves as of the Celtic Church.

The concept that a unified and peaceful Celtic Christianity existed in these islands long before the arrival of Roman Catholicism is one that was contrived in the sixteenth century by those seeking to justify the Reformation. The Protestant reformers claimed that the older church, which had been overwhelmed by Rome, was a simpler and purer form of Christianity, and therefore by rejecting Catholicism they were simply embracing an older native version of the faith.

It is understood now that this was a political argument with no foundation. The Christianity which did reach Britain and Ireland from the fifth century CE and before the spread of the Holy Roman Empire was a chaotic and fractious affair, filled with evangelical fervour and a horror of Paganism, of nature and sexuality. The idea that many Druids and Pagans were naturally and easily drawn to such a faith because it resembled their own is an extension to the myth of the purer, peaceful Celtic Church. The conversion of kings took place as an acknowledgement of a more powerful god of battle, not a move to a god of love.

For those eager to find inspiration within Christianity and through the earliest texts, the tales of the Celtic saints, men and women who struggled and succeeded in finding peace and harmony in this era of intense violence and uncertainty, are a rich source of inspiration.

The notion of Celtic Christianity is nowadays an issue quite separate from the imaginary ideal of a romantic pre-Catholicism. For many it is that part of the modern liberal Church which stands on the borderline with Druidry and Earth spirituality, acknowledging the history of these islands, bringing to the fore the saints whose faith influenced our ancestors, honouring the beauty and power of the land and seas.

*Many enter into Paganism and Druidry because of a negative attitude towards Christianity. Others avoid Druidry, believing it to be a Pagan religion. Before continuing your reading, consider where you stand on this. Where are you coming from, in terms of childhood and social conditioning, experience and beliefs? Spend some time becoming aware of your perspective.*

## THE NEXT WAVE OF INFLUENCES

For some modern Druids the old Celtic culture and the medieval literature have no direct influence on their faith whatsoever. Instead of moving back to the Celtic as a source of their Druidry, they acknowledge the later Anglo-Saxon settlers, studying their Germanic language, deities, myths and poems, and their magical tradition, with its philosophy and tools, such as the runic alphabet.

The understanding is that, if Druids were the priesthood of the Celtic people – who were the Iron Age Europeans – then the Saxons were simply a later version of the Celts. The Saxons who invaded Britain from the fifth century were still Pagan, while the Celtic kings had been Christianized, giving another reason for those who take this path to work within it. The battles between the 'red dragon' of the British Celts and the 'white dragon' of the Saxons was also one between Christianity and Paganism.

The Anglo-Saxon influence was not the only one which spread into these lands during the medieval period. The Nordic religions of the Danes, the Vikings, also made its impact, and though most who revere the Nordic gods do so through the Icelandic Asatru or Odinistic religions, there are also Druids whose principal inspiration comes through these threads.

Again, it must be understood that this is not seen as the faith of an invading force so much as simply another strand of a pan-European culture that was constantly evolving, adapting and changing with the movement of peoples. A bloodline does not remain in one location, the tribe moves on to different lands, taking its ancestral knowing, its gods and traditions with it, and – if Pagan – interweaving these forces with those of the land in which it settles.

## THE ROMANTIC REVIVAL

From the sixteenth century there came an increasing interest in antiquarianism, with a growing number of books being printed, including those of Classical writers. Images were being brought back to Britain from the colonies about the indigenous peoples of Africa and the Americas, and people were becoming interested in discovering more of their own roots.

Curiosity in the past was further generated by antiquarians such as John Aubrey, who in the late seventeenth century made a detailed study of stone monuments such as Avebury and Stonehenge. He was the first to realize that the circles were pre-Roman and, with no scientific dating system, made the connection between these sites and the Druids mentioned in Classical texts. As the eighteenth century dawned, a romantic ideal of our ancient roots was being nurtured on every level, adorned with art, poetry and music.

It was 20 years after Aubrey's death that another antiquarian, John Toland, is said to have gathered together Druids and Bards from across Britain, Ireland and Brittany for what is asserted to be the rite of inauguration of the Mother Grove of the oldest Order still in existence. Though probably mythical, this ceremony was said to have taken place on Primrose Hill, London, at the Autumn Equinox of 1717. Toland was a friend of Aubrey, who was said to be in contact with a 'Grove of Mount Haemus' in Oxford, which may also be mythical.

The successor to Toland as a key figure in the revival was William Stukeley, whose work on stone circles was influential in the development of modern archaeology, and after him came a series of eccentric men, all of whom expressed clearly the intellect of their time. Their attitude to Druidry was Christian, if Nonconformist, with a strong sense that ancient Druidry had been sent by God to prepare the ground for the coming of Christianity. The barbarism of human sacrifice was forgiven the bearded patriarchs: their faith was, after all, monotheistic, centred on the one God through the highest light, embodied in the sun.

A large swathe of modern Druidry is still influenced by the Druid revival of the eighteenth century, though for some this is underlying while for others it is a core philosophy.

In 1781, in the King's Arms public house in Poland Street, London, Toland's mythical Grove was developed into a defined Druid Order by a man called Henry Hurle. In 1834 this Order was to split into the United Ancient Order of Druids (which became the Ancient Druid Order) and the Ancient Order of Druids, both of which are still in existence.

## CULTURE AND POLITICS

By this time Scotland had lost its independence and famine crises in Ireland were inciting hatred against the English, stirring up a new Celtic spirit, while enthusiasm about ancient and cultural history was evoking an interest in all things Welsh in intellectual circles across England and Wales. It was during the eighteenth century that the modern Welsh language was created, a language which could be more easily spoken, the old Middle Welsh having been by now all but lost.

The medieval literature was also becoming more widely available. Though at this time it was mainly Welsh poetry and in poor translation, it was enough for one man, a Welsh stonemason working in London, to find the inspiration he needed.

This fellow was Edward Williams, who later took the Bardic name Iolo Morgannwg, and, returning to Wales, began to piece together all he could find about the ancient tradition. Only he didn't quite find enough to recreate the Druidry he was searching for, so with great genius and plenty of laudanum, he forged documents and poetry to validate and amplify his research. His forgeries were accepted as genuine right into this century.

In 1792, at Primrose Hill, Morgannwg assembled the first *gorsedd* (or gathering) of Bards of the Isle of Britain. Following the old Welsh tradition of eisteddfod (Welsh for a 'session' or 'sitting'), the earliest record of which is from the twelfth century, he took the *gorsedd* to Wales early in the nineteenth century.

It wasn't until 1861 that the annual national eisteddfod was again established in Wales, but it is acknowledged that Morgannwg was the inspiration behind its regeneration. Indeed, a great deal of his ritual is still used, not only within the Welsh Gorsedd, but also within many Druid Orders, both old and new.

If we look at the influence of this revival on some modern Orders, we see also the effects of attitudes which were strong around the turn of this century. The Druid groups which were prominent, most of which were all male urban societies, were by now deep into the mysticism of enlightenment. The pervading beliefs were of all religions being facets of the one religion, all gods aspects of the one God. Elements of Theosophy and the Qabala were slipping in. Sanskrit was used as freely as Welsh and Gaelic.

While these influences are for the majority of Druids unimportant or overridden, they remain hues in the spectrum of modern practice.

# WICCA AND WITCHCRAFT

The process of moving Druidry back towards Paganism was helped by the friendship during the 1950s between one of the key characters of modern Wicca, Gerald Gardner, and the Druid Ross Nichols. After disputes over leadership on the death of the previous chief of the Ancient Order of Druids, Nichols broke away to create the Order of Bards, Ovates and Druids in 1964, becoming its chosen chief. As he built the framework of the new Order, ideas he had discussed with Gardner were put into practice. The shift in focus was significant, with many more ideas slipping in that predated the eighteenth-century revival with its Christian leaning.

Perhaps the most obvious point of contrast in the spectrum of modern Druidry is where the tradition has woven its edges with Wicca and where it remains entirely separate. Over the past 30 years, many of the newer Orders have emerged through Wiccans moving into Druidry, or individuals or Groves leaving larger Orders to establish themselves with a stronger Pagan/Wiccan quality.

For some, the blend is a perfect mix of the darker, earthier energy that is felt to be Witchcraft with the lighter, clearer energy accessible through Druidry. While there are some for whom there can be no interaction, and some for whom the act of tying the two strands is seen as disrespectful to both, for many it is felt to be a natural balance between night and day, moonlight and sunshine.

There are distinct differences, however, between Wicca/Witchcraft and Druidry, though again there will be practitioners who stand in one or the other tradition yet cross the lines with which I separate them! It might be said, nonetheless, that while Wicca is a spirituality of magical practice, searching primarily for the power and energy to create change, Druidry reaches for divine inspiration, knowing that within the *awen* comes all the energy required for its expression.

The history of both traditions is equally thick with myth and fantasy, the definitions of both equally loose, enabling the seeker to create his own unique perspective and spiritual practice. However we perceive it, within the spectrum of Druidry there is a rich splash of Wiccan colour – and vice versa.

## MYTHICAL HEROES

For some in the tradition, history is a confusing mixture of fact and attitude, and felt to be best ignored in favour of the tales which appear to hold the true power of the land and the human soul.

While some dive back into the Celtic past for these tales, others prefer the kick and wit of the Arthurian sagas. To a lesser extent the other tales of our culture, such as those of Robin Hood, work within Druidry in the same way as the Arthurian.

In all these tales we can find examples of every aspect of human nature, and the Druid who walks into the inner worlds where the stories are played out in a thousand different colours and chords can merge into the characters, the landscape and the emotion, reworking the quests according to his own soul.

Not only do the stories allow us a better understanding of ourselves through whatever type of psychoanalysis we naturally employ, they also offer to the Druid archetypes of strength, glory, salvation, integrity, pride, dedication, love, and more. The kings, queens, warriors, knights, Bards, Witches and Druids, the mystical spirits and deities, all express a devotion to the land, to the people, in a way which is easily accessible on many levels.

For most, the stories inspire transformation only on a personal level, the Arthurian quest for the Grail, for example, being the

inner search for perfect release, spiritual ecstasy, the touch of the gods: *awen*. There are others, however, on the edges of modern Druid society, for whom the figures and their quests are replayed more physically as a fight for spiritual freedom and the protection of the land, through front-line environmentalism and political protest. They are a small group but their drama does at times attract attention.

## OTHER BLENDS

Not to mention the other mixes of religion within the Druid philosophy would leave a gap. In America the Order blending Hasidic Judaism with Druidry is well documented. There are a number of Druids whose spiritual practice is closer to Taoism, Shinto and Buddhism, particularly Zen, than western Paganism. While the nature of their Druidry shifts according to the concept of deity or non-deity, still the principles are there: reverence for the land and the ancestors.

There are also Druids whose inspiration comes not from conventional sources of religious teachings, but is found – with a healthy dose of humour and irony – within the science fiction stories of *Star Trek* and its genre.

## PSYCHOLOGISTS AND SHAMANS

Another distinction between Druids practising today lies within the understanding of the nature of reality.

There are an increasing number of Druids whose spiritual practice is shamanic. For these individuals there is no doubt in the existence of spirits and other planes of reality, or that the gods are existent in their own right and only vaguely affected by the desires of the human psyche. The shamanic Druid will slide between different planes of consciousness, interacting in the worlds of spirit and returning to shared reality bringing back information or having effected change.

However, a greater number within the Druid tradition do not necessarily work on this level. Some are studying ways in which shifts in consciousness can be achieved, but there are also many who do not acknowledge the worlds of spirit and the gods to be externally existent.

Understanding Druidry to be the path of deep inner healing, the way in which we relate to the spirits of the land, the spirits of nature and the ancestors is not as important as the fact that we do it. Believing that the interaction happens only within the mind, reflecting and revealing the shades of our subconscious, is as powerful a journey for many as believing that these forces exist outside and without us.

The different attitude, nonetheless, does profoundly affect the energy and practice of the individual Druid.

## ENVIRONMENTALISTS

Those within the tradition who are passionately involved in the protection of the environment come in many shapes and colours, from the road protester living through the winter in a twigloo in the forest to the organizer of an environmental awareness group or lobby to those working directly within the law on issues of pollution or development.

All within Druidry do work for the environment. For some the focus is local, for some it is global. Some are happy on a protest march, others dancing a rite within their sacred circle. However the Druid is involved, the key tenets of his faith will always guide him: we are all spirit, equal and connected.

# FOLK DRUIDRY

Over the past five years a number of Orders and Groves have worked to make Druidry more accessible to the wider public. With positive media coverage and more books being published on the subject, interest in Druidry has risen at an extraordinary rate. Not all those who get involved wish to study intensively the mysticism of the faith; many hope only to be part of a spiritual community which gathers to celebrate the cycles of the seasons and our rites of passage.

Public rituals are now increasingly being seen across the country. These are usually held during the day at sacred sites and city parks, and are open to the public, with families encouraged to attend, welcoming people of any religion (and none) to join in to whatever degree they feel comfortable.

## AND ALL FILLED WITH AWEN

The only kind of Druid not yet mentioned is the hereditary, one who claims to be of a family line through which the ancient wisdom was never lost. Whether these lines go back 40 generations or four is usually impossible to validate. It would be disrespectful to try.

Within Druidry there is no sure way of knowing whether an individual is genuine, trained and true. Few colleges or teachers issue certificates of membership, of courses completed or validated genealogies, simply because these would mean so little anyway. Knowing 300 stories in Middle Welsh is an amazing achievement and a mark of powerful dedication, but does it make a Druid? The ability to heal using energy and herbs is a divine gift, but does it make a Druid?

Becoming a Druid is a life-long task. Indeed, many say that the work of being a Druid is a constant process of becoming, of reaching the archetype of strength, wisdom, clarity, invulnerability and gentle humanity, together with an understanding of nature at its rawest edges. We stretch through our souls to the essence of life, to the spirit that vitalizes, to the gods that empower us, in search of inspiration.

Perhaps the only clear measure of a Druid, accepting that there is honour for the Earth and the ancestors, is in the expression of his *awen* ...

*Having read of the many elements and influences within modern Druidry, it is an appropriate time to consider where your inspiration comes from.*

*Which nation holds your heart, which landscape your attention? Is there an era of history that inspires curiosity, one in which you feel you would fit perhaps better than the present?*

*As you ponder on this time and place, feel the images and emotions that arise. How close are they to your present reality? How similar are the people? How much does this vision affect your present, your attitudes, your search for a spirituality?*

**PRINCIPLES OF DRUIDRY**

# THE SACRED CIRCLE

**H**aving described the history of modern Druidry and its diversity, now to offer an idea of what Druids do is a plan thick with complications. How could I possibly within these few pages reveal the nature, the flavour, the colour of every variation?

As a guide I can walk only one path at a time, though along the way I can point out other paths visible to me. The track I take is in the main that of my own Druidic practice and it is the widest track, along which the majority have made their way over the past 20 years. There will obviously be omissions, but those searching may encounter some of them, should they continue beyond these words.

## HEALING AND CONNECTEDNESS

Two clear motivations arise when looking at the reasons why people move into the Druid tradition. The first is healing, the second connectedness. Both must be taken in their broadest and most holistic sense. Yet the second, the sense of separation – from family, the wider society, our heritage, the natural world – and the desire to relieve that by reconnecting emotionally and spiritually, could also be thought of as an aspect of healing.

The potential for healing is deep and powerful within Druidry. The tradition offers an extraordinary level of inner certainty, easing any physical dis-ease or mental/emotional instability through finding a deeper sense of peace and self-confidence.

Instead of focusing on the need for light and spiritual transcendence, the Druid perspective takes us in search of spirit, finding the essence of matter, the energy within the physical that shines with life, that exists within and yet also holds the Earth and all creation. The desire is to find the point of balance, not necessarily to ensure we remain at that place, but to give us a balanced perspective and the option of equilibrium, the ability to restabilize after an adventure off centre.

Out of that search for balance comes the term 'endarkenment', asserted, with Druid humour, to steady the reaching for enlightenment. Though said with a smile, the view behind it is strong, expressing the importance within Druidry of the completeness of the natural world, of the indigo of night as well as the bright blue sky of day, the darkness of the earth and the verdancy of growth, the inevitability and release of death that shadows regeneration, the decay in autumn and growth in spring, the cycles of life and rebirth which make up the circle of being.

So our desire for understanding, for knowing, for the clarity of light, is equalled by our craving for rootedness, for achieving a deep connection and a sense of belonging in the darkness of the soil, in our land and history.

The darker, colder elements of our temperate year, the blunter aspects of nature, are reflected within our psyche, and the paths that we take in the tradition lead us through these too. As a journey of self-discovery, Druidry offers us tools to understand not only the overt sides of our nature, but also the underlying beliefs which affect us so strongly and often detrimentally.

52

In the process of changing our attitude towards the world around us, learning to acknowledge its spiritual essence and beauty, we also discover the strength and beauty within ourselves.

## SACRED TIME, SACRED SPACE

Many begin their path by creating an altar. Determining a certain place within the house or room as sacred and committing to spend time there in lives which are too busy and distracted confirms our dedication to the path. We are giving not only to all those whom we would honour at the altar, but also to ourselves. And in honouring ourselves and what nourishes us, we find ways to access more strength to interact and give out to the world.

*The art of creating and tending an altar is an important part of Druidry. It need not be big, but big enough for a candle or two and the other bits and pieces that are to be placed there. It may even be in the garden or in a secluded spot in the wild beyond.*

*Place with the candles (of any colour you choose) offerings which represent for you the beauty and strength in your life, all you would give thanks for and to, the natural world and the ancestors. It isn't necessary to make it all at once: allow it to evolve, the space itself encouraging beautiful objects to present themselves. These may be stones, shells, feathers, seedpods, cones, dried leaves or the like. You may have photos of your parents, grandparents or your children, a chalice of water, a bowl of earth.*

*The altar should be tended daily. You may bring to the altar flowers, foliage or fresh fruit, the first cookies of the batch, a hunk of bread, a little of your meal. With the candles lit, spend a period of time quietly before it. You may like to meditate, but the important part is not to let go into selflessness but to stop running, to relax, to ponder on the beauty and simply to be, for a short while, every day.*

PRINCIPLES OF DRUIDRY

*Water should be refreshed daily and any fresh food and flowers replaced when necessary (composting what you remove or leaving it in a secluded place for the wildlife outside).*

Of the sea-washed pebbles on the beach, the one we have chosen for our altar is no more blessed than the others, no more an expression of divine creation, yet picking one up, touching its smoothness, feeling its beauty, is an act of devotion, whether we understand it to have been created by a god, a natural force or a tangle of energy held within the hands of a thousand gods and spirits. Our gift to that creative force is the moment of awe which flows through us when we open our senses to the wonder of nature. It is not a feeling which can be forced, but when it fills us it makes anything but reverence for the natural world impossible. Our altar is an expression of that wonder.

So creating and working with an altar also begins the shift towards the key tenet within Druidry: that all is sacred.

The altar focuses our quest onto the natural world, but not without acknowledging the human element. As the Druid listens to the rocks and trees, she is also listening to the hum in the air, the shimmer of light and breath that holds the stories and memories of those who have walked the land before.

On our altar the photographs of our ancestors can be substituted or complemented with other symbols of what these souls have given us. Knowing that the soul is conscious between lives and actively chooses the time, place and circumstances of birth into each new lifetime, the Druid honours her parents as souls she has chosen to work with, in order to learn and grow. And our parents more often than not present us with the hardest lessons. Our children in turn have chosen us.

At difficult times in relationships the altar can be a reminder of the gifts we have been given, the opportunities for learning.

Spending a quiet moment lighting a candle for our ancestors is a potent tool for healing.

The ancestors are not only those of our bloodline. Also honoured on the altar may be a teacher or a previous resident of the house. Old pottery and flint blades found nearby may serve as reminders of the older ancestors who lived on the land before us.

Some work with an altar specifically set up for the ancestors, but for others the altar is a mix of the natural world and its human element.

The animistic vision, which sees all aspects of the created world alive with spirit, does not mean for all Druids that each stone has its gnome, each tree its dryad. Though many do interact with all creatures, rocks, flora and fungi as individual beings, the important element is not necessarily the existence of the faery folk but the way in which, as spirit, all things are connected. Every thought and action sends shivers of energy into the world around us, vibrations which affect every spirit, not only the rest of humankind and the animal realms, but all creation.

Perceiving the world as a web of connectedness helps us to overcome the feelings of separation that hold us back and cloud our vision. We are offered the certainty that we need never be alone and a language with which to communicate, spirit to spirit.

This connection with all life increases our sense of responsibility for every move, every attitude, allowing us to see clearly that each soul does indeed make a difference to the whole. It guides our understanding of how we are affected by all that surrounds us. Just as we are communicating with the world around us, so in turn it is talking to us – and as long as we are interacting only on a subconscious level we can never fully grasp it. Becoming conscious of these flows of energy, starting to hear what is being said, we slip into a different level of creative control within our reality.

## DRUID RITUAL

The sacred space of the altar and the time we spend in tending it is further extended when we look at ritual.

Ritual, playing out a prayer with a physical action, is significant. Informal ritual is a part of daily life, honouring with thanks and awe the beauty of nature, bowing with reverence to the moon as it rises, saluting the sun and stars, greeting the trees, calling to a fire sprite before lighting a match, offering thanks for food and water, blessing a soul in distress. The moments are numerous, the actions a natural response, yet often performed in a certain way, according to how the individual was taught. Where others are present ritual shows what is being done, even if words are not spoken, but more importantly it moves the body through which the energy needs to flow and through movement the subconscious mind registers change.

The ability to perform ritual more formally is an important part of the Druid's training. Within the framework of ceremony, mind and energy are concentrated and therefore stronger. A dance of words and movement is crafted which enchants the gods, evoking curiosity within the worlds of spirit, and creating opportunities for whatever transformation and regeneration are required.

### THE CALL FOR PEACE

Before any formal ritual, a call is made for peace. Addressing the four compass directions, the Druid establishes that there is peace, and if she is not alone she will also address the gathering as a whole. Why this is done has half a dozen answers, historical, traditional, romantic and psychological, as do most questions about modern Druidry.

When we call to the north, the south, east and west, 'Let there be peace!', it is a demand on our own ability both to perceive the world around us with fuller awareness and to pour into the world the beauty of peace. And, as around us, so within: the call for peace is a reminder to let go of the crises of conflict in our daily lives as we move into the sacred space of the circle.

The call for peace, then, is the first and encompassing intention of any Druid rite.

## THE CIRCLE CAST

Most formal ritual is performed within a circle that is cast and consecrated. This is the temple of the Druid. The circle is drawn on the earth or in the air, its ceiling the sky, the clouds, the trees' canopy. Many circles are cast in the same place, again and again. The most established are set with trees or stones. Neolithic stone circles are often used as modern Druid temples, while glades in the forest are considered natural sacred circles. The established circle becomes an altar in itself. Many Druids, though, will cast a circle and perform their rite, and when the circle is uncast, no trace will be left but the energy of the ceremony shimmering.

But the circle is more than simply an area marked out in which to work.

*In a place where you will not be disturbed, stand with sufficient space around you to stretch. Breathe deeply a few times, relaxing, finding your natural balance. Then bring your focus gently to the centre of that balance. In your own time, start to sense with your breathing the extent of your own space, your private space, your energy body. Some would call this the emotional body, a layer of the aura, the area around you in which you don't like strangers to linger. It may reach 10 centimetres from your skin, it may reach out to 35. It is your safe space. Trace its edge with your mind, then with a finger outstretched.*

*With the rhythm of your breath now extend that circle, pushing it out in every direction. It may be easy to do, or it may take time to find the right 'muscle'. Don't go further than is comfortable, returning often to the centre point of your balance, affirming the circle as your space, safe and certain. When you are ready, breathe it back to its original size. This may be easier, or it may take more time than extending it.*

This is a private circle and not one to share except with those we are intimate with, but understanding the circle through an exercise such as this allows us a clearer feel of what the point is, giving us a standard for what should be possible with others. A shared circle is still a place of absolute trust, though that trust is now based on the harmony between every soul present. Where there are people who don't know each other, it is the role of the Druid leading the rite to ensure that the sense of trust is shared. The act of casting the circle is an important part of this.

This is done in a number of different ways, depending on how the Druid perceives reality. By moving around the circle in a sunwise (clockwise) direction, using a pointed finger, a wand, sword or sacred knife, the Druid delineates its edge by projecting light or colour, usually of white, silver, gold or blue. More shamanically, by seeing the threads of the web of connectedness, in casting the circle the Druid will sever those threads, to refasten them again once the rite is done.

Either way, the cast circle is cut off from the world, a bubble that exists outside time and space, a perfect sanctuary. Within the circle there is no distraction or threat from the world outside, but equally importantly, the world outside is not affected by events in process within it.

**PRINCIPLES OF DRUIDRY**

# CONSECRATION

The temple of the sacred circle is usually consecrated, using incense and water which together represent the four elements the Druid works with. Within the incense is *earth*, in the dried herbs and berries, resin, bark and oils that make up the mixture which is burnt, by itself or on a charcoal block, expressing the *fire*, sending plumes of beautiful serpentine smoke into the *air*, to be breathed by the wind and the circle's participants. The *water* is often from a sacred spring, but always it is fresh, representing the waters of life. At times the chalice may have herbs or petals infusing their essence into the water.

When the circle is consecrated, the Druid calls to her gods, the elementals, the devas of the Earth, to bless the smoking censor and the chalice, then, as she moves slowly sunwise, letting the incense swirl, scattering water with fingertips, there is a shift in the energy and the vibration changes. The fifth element, *spirit*, comes into play. The circle, blessed, is ready for the rite.

## HOLDING THE BUBBLE

Working within a circle that is altogether detached from the Earth can be useful, at times, but is not the usual way within Druidry. The bubble freely floating is transcendent of the manifest world and only with lifetimes of discipline is the mind able to perfect such a temple. More often than not it bursts with the slightest touch of consciousness.

In Druidry, we bring into our temple our memories and expectations, and the bubble is held by our reverence for the world within which we live.

The Druid begins by honouring the four directions. Merely by looking at the geographic quarters – north, south, east and west – our world is created in our minds. Cultures, climates, nations and races, heat and cold, serenity and pollution, animals, colours, deserts, seas, memories of love and pain and more, all are evoked at the mention of these words. Each image rests at the edge of our focus, ready to be used.

*Take a piece of paper and a pen. Work out the directions, using the sun or a compass if necessary.*

*For a few minutes stand facing east, working out what of the Earth lies before you, which countries, which bodies of water, mountain ranges, cultures. Let your mind wander there. What do you smell? What do you feel?*

*Write down what you perceive and move on to the next quarter.*

There are no defined correspondences here, for each individual has a unique perception of the world. The calls that are made to the quarters reflect that unique vision. They are not a demand for presence or protection, but a greeting, an invitation.

So, for example, a call to the north might be:

O Spirits of the North, of the deep snows and long nights of the northern lands! O ancestors whose spirits shine bright in the starry skies! O creatures of the velvet darkness, ancient teachers of winter! Honour this our sacred rite, as we honour thee. May we feel your presence. Welcome!

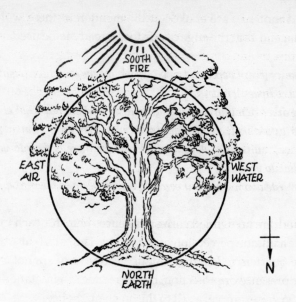

The circle sanctuary

Most in the tradition in Britain work with the four elements in the same places around the circle, with earth in the north, air in the east, fire in the south and water in the west. The calls often reflect these aspects of our world too, so a call to the east might be:

> To the spirits of the wild wind and all those who fly free upon her breath, I call to you! Feathered ones, sacred hawk, flying high on mountain air! Honoured trees who offer us our every breath of life! We ask you that you do bless this rite, in the name of the Old Gods.

By watching the images that decorate our sacred circle, we realize how constantly we project our inner vision on all that we perceive around us. Using the compass directions and the elements, then gradually seeing what else we connect with, inviting it into our sacred space, honouring its energy, we find we are offered ways to deepen our understanding of the mundane and the sacred. We find a greater clarity about what does inspire us and come closer to touching the creative force.

Once the directions have been honoured, in many Druid circles the spirits of nature are more specifically honoured, with offerings being given. The ancestors may be called, the teachers and guides who exist in spirit, with offerings of music, song, dance and drums, or a libation of wine or mead, the lighting of a candle.

Then into the temple the Druid will invoke their gods.

Druidry works as a profoundly grounded spirituality. Reverence for the natural world allows the mind and the soul to venture into the worlds of spirit knowing where it is coming from. The circle, detached from the mundane yet honouring the Earth, allows those within it to discover and affirm their strength, establish their centre, deepen their awareness of themselves and their creativity, their blocks and vulnerabilities. Rooted and blessed, reaching into the essence of life from that sacred safe space on the quest for divine inspiration, the *awen* which will pour through our bodies and souls, the spirit can truly soar.

When the ritual is completed, the devotions made and thanks given, any energy vibrant within the circle is directed according to the purpose of the rite (or some other cause) through the focus of a prayer. One often used is, 'May the world be filled with love, peace and harmony.' When the circle is uncast, the energy will flow according to the intent of that prayer.

## THE INNER AND OUTER GROVE

As well as the sacred temple in the wildwood, the individual working within the Druid tradition will also discover another

grove within the inner worlds of the mind. Some perceive this to be merely imagination, while others assert that it exists in its own right on a different layer of reality. Either way, the time spent in this grove is an important part of the Druid's work.

If we consider this to happen only in the psyche, by delving deep into the imagination to discover/create an inner temple grove we are developing the powers of our mind, expanding our ability to visualize. Both for creativity and healing, indeed any magical process, these are essential skills, and the more the student works within her inner grove, discovering its every detail, scent and colour, its patterns and sounds, moving slowly out to investigate the surrounding environment, the stronger and clearer her spiritual path becomes. The grove, like the sacred circle, is a perfect sanctuary, and finding the inner grove establishes a place which is always calm and nourishing, soul deep. Interaction with the gods and the faeryfolk, the ancestors and spirit teachers is for most people considerably easier on this inner level.

If we believe that the inner grove exists on another level of reality, every moment spent in this otherworld increases the student's knowledge and ability to function on different planes of consciousness, sliding in spirit between realities. What is gained from working on other levels differs according to the soul and the intent, but the keys are finding a radical angle of perception and potential for change. The sensual experience of being in another state can be motivation enough.

Most who study Druidry find themselves a grove outside, too. Whether they drift out there every twilight, once a moontide or twice a year, simply being out in the arms of nature, amongst the trees and in a sacred circle, is a feast to the soul.

Trees have always been important in the Druid tradition. If we slip back to an age when there were vast and ancient trees, with nothing bigger but the hills, when wood was the only source of fuel and shelter, we start to understand the reverence our ancestors had for them. In the Irish Brehon Laws of the seventh century CE trees were classified as either chieftains, peasants, shrubs or brambles, it being a capital offence to fell a chieftain tree.

The energy of trees, their spirit presence, is not always comforting. The Druid priests of yore would perhaps interpret the wisdom of the trees, appease the spirits (before the Christian priests arrived to pronounce them inanimate), as some still do. Trees can be unsettling; the great ones exist within timescales that turn humanity into scurrying mice. Catching a glimpse of such a perspective can be invaluable.

*Find a tree you feel comfortable to be with, ideally in a quiet spot where you will be undistracted. Remember to take offerings with you.*

*As you approach the tree, stop at the edge of the canopy and find once again the circle of your aura, centred in your spirit. Ask permission of the dryad before you walk into the circle of the tree. When you feel your presence has been accepted, walk slowly, aware of your energy weaving with that of the tree, circling around the trunk, spiralling in, until you find a place by the trunk appropriate for you to stay. Relax. Listen.*

*Then ask the dryad if it would be acceptable for you to raise your awareness of its being. If you feel the answer to be yes, find your balance, affirm your own circle, now interwoven with the tree spirit, lean back against the tree and close your eyes. Allow your consciousness to slide down through your body into your feet. Feel the energy of the earth holding you as it does the tree. Slip further, into the earth, so that you might feel the roots spreading out in the dark soil, drinking in moisture, holding stones, sheltering creatures. Feel the energy of the nourishment invigorating your spirit, and when you are filled let your consciousness rise up through your body, through the strength*

*of your trunk and up into your arms, reaching out like branches into the air, up to the sky, towards the light, unfurling leafbuds. Feel the sun on your face, the wind in your leaves.*

*When you are ready, slip down with your mind into the centre of your body. There, feel the balance, between Earth and sky, between sunlight and dark earth, affirming your roots, celebrating your branches, and give thanks.*

*Returning to your normal consciousness, give your offerings and thanks to the tree spirit. When you leave, detach consciously from its energy as you move out from its sacred circle of canopy and roots. Affirm your own sacred circle, your strength and connectedness.*

## OGHAM

*Ogham* is a sacred alphabet used widely within modern Druidry, where each letter corresponds to a different tree or plant. Originating from southern Ireland, it dates, some claim, from 600 BCE, but there is no evidence to prove it is any older than second century CE, with the five diphthongs being added to the first 20 letters no earlier than the late eighth century. Some excellent books on its history and potential uses, both past and present, are detailed in Chapter Nine.

There is healthy debate as to what exactly the 25 trees and plants are, with particular uncertainty over the last five. What is agreed is that each letter represents not only a tree or plant, but also a whole store of other associations, allowing the alphabet to work as a series of mnemonics. Within it are allusions to season, colour, sound, landscape, herbs, birds, insects and other wildlife, healing and toxins. Through the natural history of the trees and ancient myths, the alphabet alludes to the history of the land and its people, to politics and emotion. Indeed, nowadays there can be found tables of correspondences linking ogham to star lore, runes, other magical systems and almost anything else.

Though it may have developed as a response to the Latin alphabet arriving in Britain, ogham doesn't appear to have been much used for writing, being rather cumbersome, and for the most part is found on stone in the form of memorial inscriptions dating between the forth and eighth centuries. The last five diphthongs aren't found on any of these inscriptions, but are present in twelfth-century texts which detail the ogham alphabet with its mythology.

Many Druids feel ogham existed as an initiatory mystery, giving their ancient counterparts a way of communicating without being understood by non-initiates. Messages could be sent by a leaf or twig, or by many strung together. Letters could be signed with fingers. Complex and secret languages were developed, with ogham letter names inserted into words or syllables being replaced with ogham letter names, all in accordance with different sets of rules. Some within the Druid community use these techniques still.

With its many layers of meaning the ogham alphabet is used for the most part by modern Druids as a tool for divination, each letter opening doorways into other worlds. In the same way that runes work, their shapes can be found in landscapes, or the presence of a certain tree or plant can be understood as revealing messages and omens.

Some modern Druids who live in parts of the world where the Irish trees do not grow take the ogham and readjust it to their indigenous trees and plants. And so the tradition continues to evolve …

Druids who find their inspiration outside Ireland, meanwhile, often use the Nordic, Saxon or other rune alphabets instead. The ogham specialists tend to stand firm, however, declaring ogham the script of this land, and unsurpassable in depth and richness of meaning.

# DRUGS AND MEDICINE

The use of herbs and trees for healing, for shifting consciousness and changing the level of energy vibration, is widespread
within modern Druidry, with a significant number in the tradition qualified to work as practitioners of herbal medicine.
Many more use herbs for their own health and well-being in
preference to manufactured drugs and remedies. The hand-
making of incense is also practised within Druidry.

With an attitude that honours each plant and tree as having
its own deva or dryad, the soul seeking guidance, change or
healing will primarily address the spirit, interacting on that
level before any part of the plant or tree is physically taken or
consumed. Many Druids work solely and very successfully on
this level of relationship, spirit to spirit, sharing, releasing and
shifting, believing that any other way is unnecessarily intrusive
to both parties.

The use of illegal drugs is not encouraged in any part of
modern Druidry, not even the shamanic. It might be acknowledged that hallucinogenic drugs were taken by our ancestors in
the tradition in the same way that certain plants are still used
today in tribal religions around the world. However, most
teachers within Druidry now teach the abilities to break
through levels of consciousness, reaching trance states and
ecstasy, using just the powers of the mind.

# THE MAGICAL CYCLE

When Druids gather together their group is called a Grove, whether they meet in the forest, on the moors or in an urban setting. The Grove is a circle of souls, each honoured as individual yet sharing a common source of nourishment in the rich and fertile earth, sharing aims of growth and fruition. The branches of each soul interweave with those on either side. Each stands facing the serenity and potential of the open space which is the centre and the source.

Manifestation begins in the spirit centre of the sacred circle, moving out to the edge in the process of becoming. The flow of energy does not move in circles: it uses cycles and spirals.

## CHANGE

Change can be stressful, whether it is part of the natural process of growth and decay or something we have worked on through our creativity, our search for healing, knowing and letting go. With its focus on the natural world, its constant and inevitably changing tides, Druidry offers a tool not only for coping with change but also for thriving on it.

The Druid's sacred circle is, as we have seen, painted with the colours of his world, from his immediate environment to

68 the global geography and the universe. Though these shift and change, they are relatively still for us: trees and mountains, oceans, nations, climates. These hold us, becoming part of our perception and understanding of our world, and how within that world we can create a sanctuary, dedicated to all that has made us who we are, all that nourishes and guides us to become all that we could be ...

Into the circle are then added those elements of life which are constantly changing, all that provokes and guides us to change ourselves. The Druid temple becomes a sanctuary where change itself is blessed and contained within safe space.

## CYCLES OF TIME

Our ancestors watched the skies with awe, tracking the path of the sun, seeing how it changed through the year, observing and learning to work with the effects it had on their environment. Ancient standing stones are engraved with spirals, wheels, crescents, expressing the ancestors' fascination for the cycles of the sun, the moon, the seasons, as they lived their lives without such blinkers and blindfolds as central heating, double glazing, supermarkets and electric light. In honouring our ancestors, honouring the genetic and collective memory of lifetimes when nature was right up hard against us, day and night, winter and summer, we open ourselves to learn.

The Druid too watches the sun's path with awe. Our science may fractionally explain it, but we are still dependent on its continuity. So we watch, and learn, allowing its cycle to reflect for us the workings of our soul.

The sense of the sun being the highest light, the Logos and essence, slips into Druidry from the eighteenth-century revival. At that time patriarchal Christians asserted that Druidry had existed to prepare for the coming of Christianity, with the sun

PRINCIPLES OF DRUIDRY

holding the Truth in a similar way to the Christ-light who was to come. Where the influence of the revival is still strong there are Druids for whom the faith remains essentially a solar path, with the sun being seen as the centre and source.

While the sun/Christ connection might be interpreted as mysticism that links into many ancient schools of wisdom, for the majority within Druidry no focus on the solar is perceived, balance and integration being key tenets. None the less, the sun is the source of change in our world. Its path creates day and night and, in our temperate land, the seasons of the year.

It is our perception of these cycles which we use within the sacred circle, painting their changing colours onto the landscapes that are already there as we honour the Earth and journey into the mysteries of change.

So in the north of our circle, which we have painted with all our associated images of north and where we find the element of earth, we also acknowledge the night and all that 'night' means to us. In the north too we find winter, its cold and darkness. And in the east is dawn, spring, with its new growth waking in the tender light. In the south we honour the warmth of day, the heat of summer, and in the west we reach dusk, slipping into autumn.

In the same way that we worked with the directions and elements, by discovering the associations we hold about each season and time of day we increase our consciousness. We start to see what we hold within our subconscious in terms of memories, beliefs and expectations, all the strengths and blocks to our happiness and creativity.

The seasons not only find expression in the trees, the plants, the wild creatures of our land, the physicality of existence, but impact equally strongly upon our human psyche. In Druidry it is understood that the more closely we follow the prompts of

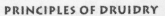

**PRINCIPLES OF DRUIDRY**

nature, releasing to the changes within ourselves, the healthier we can be. Ignoring the flows of change builds up stress and retains blinkers which deny us clarity and strength. Beyond the desire for well-being, it is in attuning with the cycles of each day and season that we discover doorways into deeper knowing, making connections with the forces of nature and the gods.

So autumn draws in and a season of growth is over, the winds taking the leaves, frost killing back the plants, and at this time we feel the need to tie up loose ends, to let go of what is redundant, to withdraw. We share with nature a death process, releasing parts of ourselves into spirit, so ground may be prepared for new life to be sown. Like the trees and perennials our focus slips from a desire to grow, our energy moving down to our roots, our sources of nourishment. The hibernation instinct creeps in.

And when spring comes we reach up into the new light, craving its touch, tender and sleepy, until the earth is warm enough for daffodils and celandines, and we are buzzing with energy, cleaning out the house and rearing to go.

Yet even here we cannot make assumptions about common ground. Each of us is unique, with an individual experience of this life and many others. For some people spring may be a time of apprehension when too much is asked of them. Summer may be a time of quiet, of avoiding the limelight, or of gallivanting through extravagant growth. For some the heat is what encourages them to open petals and stretch, while others need more water or shade. Like a grove of trees, we respond to the changing tides of life each in our own way. It is the process of becoming more conscious of who we are, discovering which tree is 'me', that allows us to begin to express ourselves more truly, evergreen yew, pale silver birch, sturdy oak, spreading chestnut …

*Where you will be undistracted, mark out a circle on the ground, physically or with your imagination. Standing in its centre, breathe gently, fully, until you are relaxed, then extend your aura until it fills the circle. Feeling its strength, the centredness of your spirit, walk around the circle's edge until you feel it is firm.*

*From the centre look around, aware of north, south, east and west, connecting the directions and elements. When you are ready, add the seasons of the year and the cycle of the day. Then, going back to the circle's edge, walk along those cycles, noting the changes that occur with every step you take. Allow yourself to feel the shifts in temperature, the changing colours and light, as you unchain your imagination and let it flow.*

*When you feel sure that your circle is marked with these cycles, return to the centre and sit quietly for a while. When you are ready, think of an emotion or a desire, such as being hungry, tired, sociable, withdrawn, creative, vulnerable, lustful, irritable, easygoing. Taking one at a time and without thinking, walk from the centre to the point on the circle's edge where you feel this state most strongly.*

*If you truly allow yourself to move without first working out where you 'should' go, the results can be surprising, revealing areas where you are sustaining stress because you are not working with your natural highs and lows. Are you forced to be in company when you would rather withdraw? Do you always call your mother at a time which is not comfortable? When would you naturally like to eat, or sleep? How do the cycles correlate, and how do these tie in to the directions and elements?*

*When you have finished the exercise, return to the centre and relax, centring yourself in your spirit energy, your strength. Then gently breathe in your aura circle until you are comfortable and give thanks to the spirits of place.*

When the Druid works in his temple, creating his sacred circle, not only does he invite the elemental energies of earth, air, fire and water to witness and empower his rite, but when he calls out to honour the directions he also calls to the spirits that embody the forces of change, to spirits of winter, spring, summer and autumn, spirits of the night, of dawn, noon and dusk.

So the circle is rich in imagery and energy, each spirit that comes giving life to the pictures in the Druid's mind, blessing the temple, offering its inspiration and power, witnessing the rite. Each spirit reveals a doorway to a different plane of consciousness through which the Druid can journey into the mists and mysteries of creation.

## MOONTIDES

To our ancestors' unaided perception both sun and moon appeared the same size in the skies. The path of the sun expanded and contracted, its power increasing and diminishing through the year, while the moon waxed to a perfect silver white circle, then waned until it disappeared into the darkness.

Little is known of how the ancient Druids worked with the moon's cycles, though there is evidence that their calendars were moon oriented. Pliny tells of Druids cutting mistletoe on the sixth day of the waxing moon. There is mention, too, of other herbs, of moon phases and the moon being a source of healing. There is imagery of gods and priests with crescent shapes assumed to be lunar symbols.

For those practising Druidry today, the moon is equal in importance to the sun and as many rites are held at night, in the flickering light of the fire, as are held during the daytime. There is no emphasis on the full or dark (new) moon in the tradition and the majority of Druids tend only to gather together for the major festivals of the year, preferring to honour the lunar tides on their own. However, there are Groves which meet at the full or dark moon, while some meet on the sixth day and at the waning quarter.

Understanding the relationship between sun, moon and Earth is a source for much spiritual adventure, intriguing modern Druids, who are less likely than those of other traditions to follow any specific convention. What is the relationship between light, dark and bright, between source, reflection and perception, between reason, emotion and actuality, body, soul and spirit?

Though for many the sun is perceived to be a male force and the moon female, this is not always the case, either in traditional mythology or in modern practice. It is up to each individual to create and nurture his own unique relationship with the spirit energy of sun and moon, as with all the world around him and the souls and deities which inspirit that world.

In the same way that the sun's cycle was laid upon the edge of the sacred circle, so too the tides of the moon find their place. These vary according to how comfortable the Druid is with the various times of the lunar month. The most common form is where the phases are aligned with the cross quarter points, halfway between the cardinal directions.

This gives us the dark moon in the north-west, when the power of sun and moon are aligned before us, intensifying our experience, as we walk towards winter. The first quarter is placed in the north-east, where we find the snowdrops and the first hints of dawn. The full moon is in the south-east, when the moon is on one side and the sun lies directly opposite, pulling us this way and that in a frenzy of paradox and creativity. The waning quarter is in the south-west, as the harvest begins. Laying the moon phases in this way emphasizes the language of change that the lunar cycle offers us.

# STAR MARKERS

By the time the Celts reached Britain in the first millennium BCE the climate was not conducive to starwatching, the religious focus having shifted from the skies to water as wet weather became the norm. None the less for many Druids there is a strong connection between their faith and the ancient tombs, standing stones and circles that align with the rising and setting of the sun, moon and various stars. In the medieval texts there are implications that the Druids still knew their star lore and the mysteries of the skies, and certainly many in the tradition today are accomplished students of astrology, astronomy and astro-alignment.

Few in Druidry, however, practise in a high ceremonial style where the exact positions of stars are required in order to perform rites. For the modern Druid the science of nature is not used to strengthen the intellect in order to defend ourselves against it, the goal being rather to attune with nature, slide in and extend our experience of its reality. Stars are considered to be omens and guides rather than dictators of fate, our observation being an act of reverential awe and learning.

Aspects of astrology relate well into modern Druidry, such as the use of the elements of earth, air, fire and water, each being further qualified by the term cardinal, fixed or mutable, bringing in qualities of change. The importance of balance is shared, with the focus on relationship, integration and healing through a strong vision of connection. The pathways of change are clearly mapped out, from the circle of the horizon to the elliptic voyages of planets and stars.

The importance of 'now' is explored through star lore, that gap between time and space, between past and future, the intangibility of the present moment which is captured in the sacred circle. The Druid strives to understand more fully all the energies – of the planets, stars, moons, gravity – which influence our journey. As through spirit every aspect of our world is connected, so the stars breathe their energy over our Earth through a cosmic web of connectedness.

Many Druids understand the skies sufficiently to work with the stars, constellations and planets as they change throughout the year, painting them into the changing colours of their temples and devotions.

There are Druids who create circles of standing stones, trilithons and labyrinths, aligning them with the rising and setting of celestial bodies, some building temples to predict eclipses in the way that the neolithic architects perfected. So it is that new sacred places are emerging and the tradition continues to evolve.

## BIRTH TO DEATH

The cycle of life is also played out within the sacred circle, its shades and tones painted onto the circle's edge. So, as the sun begins its new journey in the depths of darkness at Midwinter, the new soul comes into life.

When the sun begins to rise higher, warming the earth, and shoots creep through the soil, sap moves back up from the roots, so the infant grows into the child and with spring he emerges from the enfolds of his mother, exploring further and further from her protective, nurturing space. Childhood adventures, growing consciousness and the development of independence are encompassed in the east. Adolescence takes us down towards the circle's south-east, where fertility and sexuality rise to a peak. In the south is the height of our physical expression, our asserted creativity, where fire brings us courage, power and energy. Here is our adult life, which after Midsummer shifts towards middle age, when the harvest is

ripe and drying in the sun. As we move into the west, the emphasis on the physical is replaced by the importance of experience, wisdom and balance, the autumn leaves falling inevitably and with such exquisite beauty. As the trees stand bare and the darkness comes in, the last period of our lives takes us into winter where death awaits us. At Midwinter we are reborn.

Attuning to the cycles of the natural world mirrors for us the cycle of our own lifespan. It reveals for us our perceptions and expectations of life, offering doorways of healing and adventure.

## PATHS OF THE CIRCLE

It isn't only the path around the edge of the sacred circle which is used by the Druid. There are pathways that reach across the centre, taking us down lines of reflection and connection, and these paths too are ritually trodden. Walking the paths when wholly focused within the temple circle the seeker is guided to poignant opportunities for healing.

In the east, for example, the child looks over to the west, where the elder speaks his wisdom. In the west, as age creeps in, the soul looks to the child for a vision of freedom. In the south-east, where sexuality is humming, the couple looking for fertility see across the circle the end of life and they acknowledge their ancestors in the north-west as they strive to create a space for their descendants. The activity and physicality of the ever shifting, doing, flickering fire of the south reflects the north, its solidity, physical being, rooted firm. The adult who stands taking on the responsibilities of the community, committing to his direction, bringing in the harvest in the south-west, is reflected by the young child of the north-east struggling to cope with his first steps out of dependence.

The southern half of the circle is warm, light, filled with action, growing outwards, while the northern half is dark, cold, deep, a time of integration, consolidation, nourishment. For some the energy of air and fire, wind and sun, are more masculine, whereas the water and earth, the tidal womb energy, are feminine. Another line can be drawn between the times of growing, from the Midwinter birth of the new Sun Child in the north to the point in the south where the year turns at Midsummer, bringing us back through the season of release and decay.

Just as places around the edge of the circle act as gateways into the deeper mysteries of the human psyche, places where we can access our inspiration, marker points which take us through into different planes of reality, so the paths across the circle do the same. It is in the centre that we are balanced, but it is the journeys we make through life that take us to the cutting edges of our soul, where we grow in knowledge, beauty and certainty, where we meet our gods and spirit guides and through communion reach ecstasy and freedom.

## ANIMAL LORE

The spirits of the trees, shrubs and herbs that encircle our grove hold our energy, teach and inspire us, but it is the animal spirits who move through our sacred places that lead us into different worlds and levels of consciousness.

Druidry is rich with teachings and guidance about the connections between the human soul and the animals around us. Many in the tradition work with animals, both in spirit and in flesh, fur, feather and fin. As the Druid watches and listens, relaxing, open to possibilities, an animal will often stride, creep, hop, skid or fly into consecrated space, or appear upon the pathway of his life or inner journeys. Sometimes it is just one, but it can be a number or many different animals, each taking a different role, aiding the Druid on his way.

Some animals work simply as guides, enabling the Druid to expand his view of reality and travel further into other worlds. These guides might remain for a while and then become elusive or disappear. Others connect more deeply with the soul of the Druid and are known as totems. The totem animal will be one which has worked with the individual over many lives, remaining as an integral part of her soul's experience. Some totems are linked with bloodlines or soul families (groups of souls who repeatedly incarnate together), while a person who is born into a family group where his totem animal is not comfortable will always feel alienated until he finds others of his totem clan.

There are many Druids who work with a particular animal by caring for one as a companion, such as a cat. Many campaign for the protection of totem wolves, bats, bears, lynx, eagles and so on.

As the Druid calls to the directions, inviting spirits to guide, bless and inspire the rite, invoking spirits of the seasons, elements, night and day, so he also calls to the animals with whom he works.

Many animals may (in body or in spirit) already be present in the circle, settling where they wish, while others are invited to the grove, bringing with them their unique strengths and teachings.

So a call to the south might be:

> In the name of the great stag in the heat of the rut, may this ceremony be blessed with the powers of the south!

Or a fuller call to the west might be:

> Powers of the west, I call upon you, spirits of the ocean deep, of cleansing rain and healing tears! Ancient salmon who swims in

the sacred pool of wisdom, I ask for your blessing of inspiration
on this our rite! As we honour you, so may it be!

It is easy to lay down guidelines as to where the animals of
our world might find themselves in the sacred circle, with the
feathered folk in the east with air, the water folk in the west,
the wild creatures of the greatest strength and ferocity in the
south and those of the night in the north. Yet no set of correspondences can strictly apply. For some the fox is always a
creature of the south, with flame-coloured brush and sparkling
eyes, while to others he is a night animal of the north. For some
the eagle is a creature of the east, playing on the high winds,
while for others he flies as a messenger of the sun and resides in
the southern quarter. Other animals will not rest in any particular place within a circle, behaving indeed rather more like
animals than figments of the imagination.

Some Druids only work with animals native to where they
live, while others slip through soul memories to invoke spirits
of other lands and times. The individual finds his own sources
of spiritual and creative inspiration, his unique inner landscape. When Druids gather, the animals called into the circle
tend to be those of a shared reality of myth and landscape, of
the Earth beneath their feet.

But how *does* an animal guide?

Through relaxing, listening, the soul working in the tradition slowly forms a relationship with an animal, making offerings, learning the language of spirit which both share. The
seeker begins to see the creature in a new way, its movements,
reactions, noises, all suggesting answers to the questions
which are the current focus. The Druid might hear the voice of
the creature in spirit, communicating its perspective, and
through learning to access a profound level of empathy he

slips into that position to look at the world from the animal's point of view.

One step further takes the Druid into shapeshifting. Beginning with the imagination, finding the freedom for a moment to join the hawk gliding over the trees, the further end of the spectrum can take the Druid to where his consciousness moves entirely into another state, believing his body to have changed. Not only is the human body replaced with that of the animal, but so is the mentality. Many Druids find this is possible to varying degrees with their totem animals, some finding it immeasurably valuable for their spiritual development, inner freedom and ability to help and heal the worlds within which they live.

Each animal has its own strengths, its own outlook, its own natural lore, offering us ways through the blocks in our human self-consciousness.

For example, dogs are known for their loyalty, their understanding of leadership and rightful place in the pack, the energy that they give to the hierarchy, all qualities which can be useful or self-negating. Through a relationship forged with a dog we find these aspects within ourselves, allowing a deeper healing, and offering healing to the dog through gratitude and respect. The horse teaches us of cooperation, speed, journeying, feeling the land. The swan shows us the balance between elegance and hard work, love, death and memory. The blackbird guides us through the changes of dawn and dusk, its enchanting call taking us into magical places of intangible beauty. Cats teach of independence, frogs of cleansing, otters of laughter, and so it goes on.

The most poignant and instructive way of discovering the qualities of any creature is to observe it in its natural environment – or as close to it as is possible to get. Studying books on its nature, diet, relationships and habitat are a beginning, followed by those where it is present in folk stories, history and mythology.

No animal is of lesser or grander status than any other. The wren is as potent an ally as the eagle, the wood pigeon as deeply magical as the hawk, each giving a different vision, different doorways through which we might step.

Creatures which are feared or reviled in our culture or mythology are often very powerful allies, guiding us through phobias and crises of our own strength and worth. The wolves, snakes, rats, bats and spiders who wander through our inner worlds trigger some of the most powerful imagery and journeys with so much emotion around them suppressed within our souls. These creatures are often associated with issues around death and sexuality.

If we request of the gods that an ally be sent us, one we might learn from and find healing, then whatever comes will in one way or another offer just that.

*Finding a animal ally is a useful ability and a simple one to grasp. In your own sacred space, having cast the circle of your aura and let go of distractions, find that state of being relaxed, listening. Become aware of yourself, how your emotions have coloured life recently, and consider what quality you would benefit from now. Strength, protection, calm, courage, playfulness … Then invite that quality to enter your circle in the form of an animal and let it happen in its own time.*

*Welcoming the creature, give offerings of thanks. Feel its energy. It is now up to you to nurture your relationship and learn from it.*

# THE CELEBRATION

The importance of celebration in Druidry cannot be overstated. Eight major festivals celebrate the cycle of the year and, if rites of passage that mark important events in our lives are not woven into a festival rite, another celebration is declared to honour these too. Both are an expression of wonder at the natural world, enabling each soul more powerfully to attune to the significance of every step along the way.

Celebration strongly marks the importance of community. Though some in the tradition celebrate the festivals alone, an increasing number congregate, affirming the power of their rite and sharing laughter, strength and teachings. The community is drawn together, witnessing the passing of time and the changes it brings, and assuring mutual support. Rites of passage are witnessed – dedications, vows and thanksgivings.

The family is honoured in Druidry and many open gatherings actively welcome children. Some insist that they behave respectfully when they reach a certain age, this being an important part of the child's education about the faith. In a tradition which holds strongly the tenet of honouring the ancestors, the children – our descendants – are also honoured, invited to share and find their place within our society, taking responsibility, finding pride in their heritage, connection with the land, certainty and self-esteem.

Time is also allowed for adult ceremonies when, with no children present, the energy can be more intense.

Creativity comes into its own at festival celebrations, which usually include at least one eisteddfod. At *gorseddau*, gatherings of Bards, the eisteddfod is an integral part of the festivities. At an eisteddfod any person wishing to share the results of her *awen*, her divine inspiration, is given the circle centre to perform. The most usual forms of expression are music, song, storytelling and poetry.

## THE DRUID CALENDAR

The Druids' command of astronomy was famous throughout the ancient world, bringing a knowledge of nature's cycles and sufficient information to create a calendar through which they might establish some certainty about celestial events, from the pathways of the sun and moon to eclipses and stellar patterns. Maintaining this information at an initiatory level, without committing it to writing, would have been another element that allowed Druids to maintain their élite position in society.

As a result, little information has reached us, though we are told in the Classical texts that Druids measured time by the moon and by nights, not days. This is shown on the one calendar which did survive, a bronze tablet 2,000 years old, found a century ago in Coligny, central France. A table of religious festivals, it marks auspicious and inauspicious days spanning a five-year period, and would almost certainly have been crafted on Druids' advice.

There is no evidence that the Celtic people marked the solstices or equinoxes with celebration, nor are these solar events mentioned in the Welsh or Irish medieval texts. It is in the alignments of megalithic structures built by the predecessors of the Celts that we find a focus on these dates. West Kennet Long Barrow in Wiltshire, for example, has an equinoctial alignment. The Winter Solstice is marked at the developed passage graves of Newgrange in Ireland and Maes Howe in the Orkneys, while Stonehenge has a prominent Midsummer alignment. The different focus of temples and tombs suggests either that people travelled to different locations to celebrate events or that local groups observed different nights or days.

So what are the festivals celebrated by modern Druids?

The wheel of eight festivals was brought to Druidry by Ross Nichols who, in the late 1940s, was a member of the Ancient Druid Order, which at the time was celebrating only the two equinoxes and the Summer Solstice. Rumour has it that they would have marked the Winter Solstice too but the weather was a disincentive. During his research into Irish folklore Nichols came across the festivals of Samhain, Imbolc, Beltane and Lughnasadh and decided that these ought to be brought into modern Druidry.

When his idea was rejected by the hierarchy of the ADO, he showed his mandala of festivals to his friend Gerald Gardner. Gardner, who was in the process of putting together the elements of modern Wicca, immediately incorporated it into his ideas. His coven was presumably the first to put it into practice in the early 1950s, while Nichols had to wait until 1964, when he led a breakaway group from the ADO to form the Order of Bards, Ovates and Druids.

The wheel flows so beautifully, every six weeks or so marking a point in the cycle of changing, bringing the community together, bringing our consciousness to presence, that many newcomers to the tradition find it hard to believe it hasn't always been that way.

# THE FESTIVALS OF THE SUN

To modern Druids the eight holy days are all equally important, though media attention and public ritual have brought the focus onto the Summer Solstice perhaps more than any other. The time of the 'highest light' does draw attention, particularly in our temperate and temperamental climate.

Establishing a calendar at the latitude of the British Isles is best effected by the sun, watching the clear stretch in its path through the year from winter to summer. While other calendars may be created by the rising and setting of more distant stars, our climate doesn't allow such reliable sky watching. The dramatic shifts in light and temperature we experience through the year direct our focus to the sun, the source of the change, the centre of our circling world's view.

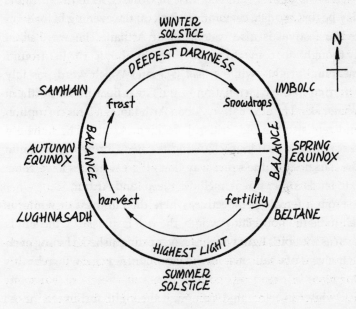

The cycle of the year

In our cool temperate climate it is the rebirth of the sun at Midwinter, when the days start to get longer, that is seen by many in the tradition as the time of greatest celebration and this festival has grown and grown; the Winter Solstice is now blurred in many non-Pagan minds with the commercial exuberance of Christmas. The instinctive relief that the days are getting longer, that darkness has reached its peak, floods through the festival, secular, Christian and Pagan. Our Germanic ancestors, who called the festival Yule, established the tradition of celebrating for 12 days – another aspect of Paganism taken up by Christianity.

In Druidry the Winter Solstice is celebrated around 21 December, when the sun enters Capricorn, or three days later on the date we call Midwinter, 24 December, when after a pause at its lowest point the sun once again starts its journey back towards the centre. Because in Druidry, as in Judaism, the day begins at dusk, celebrations kick off the evening before.

The festival is also called Alban Arthan. The word *alban* is thought to come from an early Brythonic (British) word meaning 'bright', while *arthan* is a later Welsh word possibly referring to the constellation of the Great Bear in the northern winter sky. The alternative, Alban Arthuan, is a later corruption and refers to the old British hero king, Arthur. The newborn sun returns as saviour, changing the tides, bringing light into the darkness, in the same way that all great heroes have come into lands under threat, including Jesus and Arthur.

From a female perspective, where the darkness of winter is felt to be the nourishing womb, the rich fertile earth, the sun is seen as the spirit light which is never extinguished, shining even in the void of death, inspiring conception, new growth, rebirth.

Midwinter is celebrated, as are all the eight and indeed most rites in the tradition, with a ceremony held within the temple sanctuary of stones or wood or simply energy, where peace is affirmed and the circle cast, consecrated and blessed, and into which are invited the spirit presences, the ancestors and deities, with whom the Grove normally work.

The heart of the ceremony is the ritual ending of mourning for the death of the light, in whatever godform or abstract that is perceived. The year which was drawn to its close with the onset of winter, bringing with it the chaos and uncertainty of darkness, is now left behind. The miracle of birth has stopped the running flow into the darkness: the tide is turned.

A new world is emerging, albeit still enfolded in the arms of its dark mother, and her energy still surrounds us. With reverence we acknowledge her being and her gift, the infant light. The Spirit Child is reborn and all who have gathered in sacred space honour his arrival with wonder, bringing vows of dedication together with offerings of their own spirit, strength and beauty.

Folk customs may be incorporated into the ceremony or brought to the celebrations around the fire and the feast afterwards, depending on what is local or appropriate, including the burning of the winter oak log symbolizing the spirit of the hearth fires that warm the community. Mistletoe is distributed, carrying its magical blessings of healing, fertility and presence. Boughs of evergreen decorate the house, holding the spirit of life through the dark winter months. Presents are given, expressing the energy of our spirit, honouring the new year that is born and affirming bonds of love and community.

This is often an intimate celebration, in the heart of winter when few will or can travel far, a time of caring, sharing and feasting with our close friends and family around us.

# SPRING EQUINOX

The Spring Equinox is celebrated between 20 and 23 March, on the date when the sun moves into Aries and day is the same length as night. It is also known as term Alban Eilir, sometimes written as Eiler, *eilir* being Welsh for 'regeneration' or 'spring'. Alban Eiler is translated poetically as 'Light of the Earth'.

Christian tradition has again used many Pagan symbols evident in Eilir celebrations, although in Christianity the festival is aligned with the Judaic Passover and called Easter. The Germanic name for this Pagan celebration is Ostara. This is the name of a fertility goddess and comes from the same root as the word 'Easter', as do the words 'oestrus' and 'oestrogen'.

The equinox is a time of new life, daffodils and cherry blossom, fledglings, lambs running in the fields. The symbolism of the egg is prominent. It is a time of celebration of childhood, with games to be played.

This is another turning point in the year, not across a peak but across a point of balance. The darkness is behind us and ahead is the light into which we can grow. As with the Autumn Equinox, many who are sensitive to the energy of the cycle feel drawn into the balance over a few weeks before and after the actual date, as if the process of settling is unsettling in itself. At the Spring Equinox this is particularly difficult, with the energy running fast and increasing all the time. The sap is rising.

The core of the Eilir ceremony is the blessing of seeds that will become the year's harvest. On a practical level within the rite, seeds might be blessed and sown in pots that will be cared for on windowsills or in greenhouses, protected still from the frosts. While these seeds will usually be a part of the work of caring for the land which the Druid takes part in through the year, they also represent other projects. They are ritually blessed with the elemental forces of flowing breath air, of sun fire warmth, of moisture and rain and, of course, rich soil earth, an act which simultaneously blesses those plans which we are beginning to put into action, consecrating them with elemental strengths – our intellect and knowing, courage and energy, intuition and motivation, and our ability to stabilize and manifest.

Now the Sun Child has grown and his heat is touching the Earth, drawing us up into growth. In the rite this is often played out by the spring maiden and young sun god, aware of their sexuality yet not old enough to use it. They dance, not touching, shy and innocent, filled with the energy of life renewed.

The tides are high, the moon is large and bright. Eilir is a festival filled with laughter and anticipation, excitement for the growth ahead as the balance tips towards the light.

## MIDSUMMER

The Summer Solstice is the festival most often associated with Druids, though it is of no more importance in the tradition than any other festival. It is celebrated around 21 June when the sun rises at its most northern point, climbing highest in the sky, as it passes from Gemini into Cancer, or on Midsummer's Day three days later on 24 June, after the pause when the sun begins its descent.

The festival is also known as Alban Hefin, sometimes written as Heruin, the Welsh word *hefin* meaning 'summer'. Alban Heruin is referred to as 'Light of the Shore'.

The festival is a celebration of the peak, and the further north we travel the more potent is this rite. The sun born at Midwinter has pushed back the powers of darkness to just a few night hours. But in the process he has exhausted himself (in many solar myths he is wounded in the fight) and it is at this point that his hold relaxes. Darkness once again begins to creep silently in.

The interplay of the forces of nature continues, weaving threads of tension, life and death, dark and light, male and female, pushing and pulling. If Midwinter is about the power of the dark feminine, the shrine of the womb, the deep valley, the cauldron, the 'inner' and receptive, then Midsummer is a time of honouring the power of the light, the masculine, the mountain top, the sword's blade, the outer and assertive. Both qualities exist within every soul and are expressed in the changing flows of life; at Hefin we acknowledge the outward expression of ourselves, our vitality and strength, all we have used in the push for growth and progress, and we learn when to stop.

The celebrations for Alban Hefin often begin at dusk the evening before and include three distinct parts: the rite that initiates the night vigil, the rite of dawn and that of noon. There is high celebration of the power of the Sun King, often enacted through the replaying of a myth. Thanks and honour are given, and dedications made to the power and glory of the solar deity, saviour, hero. Through the night vigil the eisteddfod keeps the focus strong and laughter loud, and at dawn the power of the sun is honoured with awe and offerings. At noon the rite changes, as the turning tide is acknowledged. Teachings are shared of the need to balance power with justice, strength with wisdom. Our attention is drawn from the light that glints off the sword to the Earth, the goddess of our land.

As with all the festivals there is a mine of folklore connected to Midsummer. Though the sources of much of this are lost in the mists of time, there is good literary evidence that the ancient Celts of France and Wales celebrated Midsummer by rolling burning wheels down hillsides from great hilltop fires. Divination was common practice at this time.

The Autumn Equinox is celebrated between 20 and 23 September, when the night is as long as the day once again and our sun star slips in front of the constellation Libra. Also known as Alban Elfed, sometimes written as Alban Elued, *elfed* meaning 'autumn', it is translated as 'Light of the Water'.

The balance is more poignant at this time than in the rush of spring and this is often the quietest of the festivals. The harvest is in; it is a time of acceptance of all we have and what we lack, a time of reflection on what we have achieved. The element of water is strong, the ebb and flow of the ocean tide, as we stand in the west of our sacred circle, reaching out to understand the mysteries of balance. This is a time of sharing gifts of abundance and strength, a time when participants bring to the rite offerings and presents for each other and the gods.

At many Groves it is usual to bless and share food and drink at all the festival rites. This is often in the form of a large round loaf of homebaked bread and honey mead (or cider, ale or wine) passed around the circle in a drinking horn. After giving thanks to the goddess of the land and to the lord of light, and acknowledging the alchemy that transforms the grain into bread and blossom's nectar into mead, the gathering will ask for their blessings on the loaf and the horn. The first break of bread, the first drink of mead are given back to the land, to Mother Earth, the spirits of place, and if appropriate for the rite more is given to the ancestors through the flames of the fire.

If a Grove does not celebrate this feast at every rite, most will do so at the Harvest Equinox.

## THE FESTIVALS OF THE SEASONS

While the solar festivals are fixed points in the cycle of the year, the other four mark the opening of a season. The energy of each

92    of these festivals is evident throughout the three months that
follow until the next one looms, altered by the solar turning
point in the middle. Within Pagan Druidry, the seasonal festivals are most commonly known by the Irish Gaelic names
Samhain, Imbolc, Beltane and Lughnasadh. They are also
known as quarter days or lunar or fire festivals.

These festivals are not defined by precise cosmic events, but
by the cycle of nature herself, by the dance of the weather gods
and spirits of place. They require us not to look to the heavens
but to the Earth. They are set within our soul, watching the
leaves on the trees, the animals, insects, birds, feeling the shifting temperature, the changing light, within and around.

## SAMHAIN

Though the spelling of the Irish varies the pronunciation tends to
stay the same, so Samhain is also seen as Samhuinn and Samain
but is spoken as *sow-inn*. The meaning is probably 'Summer's
End'. The Welsh name is Calan Gaeaf, meaning 'Winter Calends'.

For those who measure by the seasons, Samhain arrives
with the first frost. Some plan their rite around the full moon of
Scorpio that passes through Taurus. Those who work around a
consistent date celebrate Samhain on 1 November, with the
rites beginning the evening before. The Pagan festival has been
overlaid nowadays by both the Christian All Hallows, All
Souls and All Saints and the secular Guy Fawkes.

Medieval texts imply that Samhain was the most important
festival in Ireland, a time when laws were made and kings
instated. Yet also it was a time of madness and danger, when
monsters caused havoc and faery women bewitched young
men, enchanting them away. *The Yellow Book of Lecan* refers to
Samhain as 'the feast of Mongfind', a legendary witch queen
said to have married an early high king of Tara, which implies
that she was an incarnation of the spirit of the land.

Traditionally at Samhain, livestock that would not last the winter were slaughtered with ritual thanks. Meat would be cured, salted, put aside, and the tables of the feast laden with bloodcake and offal which could not be preserved, together with the blackberries and fruit of late autumn.

Samhain marks the end of summer and a cycle of growth. It is a time of sacrifice.

Ahead is the winter and decisions need to be made as to what we will carry through the long cold months, what is redundant, what will not survive, and what must be protected and nurtured as the source of next year's wealth.

So the festival rite is a process of letting go, beginning with an acknowledgement of what we have gained, how we have changed and who we have become, and followed by a period of mourning, knowing what we must release – and effectively letting it go. The past is gone.

At this time, those who have died during the year are honoured and gifts are given with love and thanks, perhaps with candles being lit and set to drift on water, symbolizing the journey travelled by the dead over the ocean to the place of the setting sun. That journey between the worlds, between life and death, is at Samhain most easily made.

Our ancestors who would join the rite in peace are invited to share and the feast is blessed and offered to the Earth, the spirits and all in the circle.

Then the darkness of winter is welcomed in and a period of release is declared when chaos is accepted. From this tradition trick o'treating was reintroduced. Now bonfires are lit, the Summer King burnt, fireworks set off – and the feasting begins.

# IMBOLC

Imbolc or Imbolg, by the calendar, is celebrated on 2 February. Pronounced *im-olk*, it is thought to refer to the ewes' milk which flows as lambs are born. Some mark the time of Imbolc by the birth of the first lambs, while others look for the first snowdrops. To some it is the festival of the full moon of Aquarius which passes before the constellation of Leo.

In Welsh the festival is known as Gwyl Fair, 'The Feast of Mary', or the newer alternative Gwyl Forwyn, 'The Feast of the Virgin', though some Druids, even the Pagan, use the Christian term Candlemas. In Ireland and parts of Scotland it is the festival of Brigit, Bride or Brighid, an ancient goddess whose worship was transferred to a Christian saint.

This is the first festival of spring, when the Sun Child born in the depths of winter lifts his face and the Earth is touched with the first rays of warmth. The fire of Imbolc is the tender light of new life that flickers in the candles of the rite, the forge of the metal-working goddess who cleanses and re-forms our souls ready for the year ahead, the fire of poetic inspiration.

For many Druids Imbolc is the only festival entirely focused on the feminine deity and the rite is often powerfully gentle, woven with poetry, the circle veiled in white, expressing the innocence of the child. At this time we honour our mothers, and our mothers' mothers, with offerings of thanks to all who have given us life. Plans are shared, our aspirations and dreams, still abstract and wrapped in hope. White candles, planted in a cauldron of earth or water (symbolizing the body of the goddess or the waters of the womb), are blessed and lit, infused with our love, devotion, dreams and prayers.

The spelling of this festival varies from Belteinne to Bealtine, the most common being Beltane, which is closest to its pronunciation. The word can be translated as 'the bright (or fortunate) fire' and some make the connection with the Irish Balor, the Gallic god Belenus and the Welsh Beli Mawr, all ancestral deities associated with light and fire. This is the first festival of summer, celebrated by the calendar on 1 May, with the rites beginning the previous evening, or on the full moon of Taurus as it passes through Scorpio. Those who mark their quarter days by the flows of nature celebrate with the first pinky white blossoms of the hawthorn tree, also known as the may.

In Welsh it is Calan Mai, 'The Calends of May', and in Welsh medieval literature many important events take place at this time. The date features in the same way that Samhain does in the Irish tradition, with demons stealing newborn children, dragons fighting each other and the gates to the faery realm standing dangerously open.

In the Irish literature we are told that the old gods, the Tuatha de Danaan, arrived in Ireland at Beltane. *Cormac's Glossary* (of around 900 CE) relates that all fires were extinguished at Beltane, to be rekindled from those lit by Druids who chanted spells over them, infusing them with magical properties, and cattle were driven between twin fires on hilltops as a charm against disease before being led to their summer pastures.

The Beltane rite in modern Druidry focuses on fertility: for those wanting children, for the land, farmed and wild, for our own souls and dreams. The twin fires of the rite express the duality of nature, the tension of opposites craving union, the source of creativity.

The Earth has come alive now with energy bright and strong; the air is humming, filled with the scent of flowers; the forest is

green once more. The young Sun King and the Spring Maiden have grown to sexual maturity and the ritual is the dance of their coming together. She is now the May Queen, with a crown of hawthorn, and he comes to her as the Lord of the Wildwood, the green man dressed in leaves or the sun god himself. Their dance is infectious and they leap the fires, blessing them with fertility, creativity and good fortune, encouraging all who have gathered to leap the flames and be blessed.

There are many folk customs around Beltane, such as washing one's face with dew before dawn to bring beauty, picking certain herbs said to inspire attraction, blessing the bees who give us mead, the dance around the May pole, and the disappearing of couples into the forest and fields to make love in the moonlight. It is a time of music and dance, youthful energy and freedom.

## LUGHNASADH

Lughnasadh, Lughnasad or Lugnasa, pronounced *loo-nass-ah*, is the festival of the god Lugh. In medieval Irish texts it is also referred to as Bron Trogain, or the first day of the Trogain month, and is now commonly known as Lammas, the Saxon word meaning 'loaf mass', or by the Welsh term Gwyl Awst, meaning 'The Feast of August'. The third festival of summer, it is the celebration of the first harvest of our local staple grain, usually wheat or barley. Some hold their rites on the full moon of Leo as it passes through Aquarius. By the calendar Lughnasadh is 1 August.

However the festival was celebrated, and it appears to have differed across Britain and Ireland, it was always the celebration of the first fruits of the harvest. There were fairs (the most documented being at Tailtin/Teltown in Ireland), the making of straw figures, the dressing or decoration of wells with prayers, horse races and other games. Those in search of work would be hired for the year, rents and other legal disputes would be settled, and marriages made.

The season of growth since Beltane has come to its end and now we enter the season of reaping. Myths are often played out during the Lughnasadh rites, with the Corn King offering himself up to be sacrificed and being reborn as the loaf of newly baked bread. The grain is also taken to make ale and the straw is used for bedding through the winter to come. The summer is waning. The power of the sun god has been given into the yellow corn.

The sacrifice of the king was at one time very real, as blood was offered back to the gods who had given the grain. The focus of the rite now is still this weave of exuberant life and release to death. It is both a celebration of what we have sown and nurtured, which has now come to fruition, and an acknowledgement of its dying as it dries in the heat of summer, giving itself up to our needs. The hard work of harvesting must be done, with acceptance of our responsibility for gathering it in. After the grain the dark fruits and berries will ripen, bringing an altogether different energy to the feasts to come.

Lughnasadh is often the biggest of the festivals, with people travelling from far and wide to share the joys of their harvest, bringing music and food, and trading crafts and stories.

*One of the festivals will be coming up in the next month or so from the time of your reading this chapter. Which one is it? What season are we in? What is happening to the energy of the land and how does that relate to the energy of your body and soul? How would you like to celebrate the coming festival?*

# RITES OF PASSAGE

The cycle of festivals allows us to take distinct steps through the year, acknowledging the changes and our own progress every six weeks. It is also felt necessary within the tradition to make clear statements of our progress through the cycle of our lives. So the Druid family is offered rites of passage which carry the members from conception to death. These ceremonies of celebration, dedication and transformation are to some extent individually crafted to be specifically relevant to the people involved. They are designed to aid processes of change, to bring confidence and affirm support.

The newly conceived foetus is blessed, the newborn child welcomed and formally named, and in both rites the mother, father, grandparents and ancestors are honoured. Children are blessed with the falling of their first tooth and at other stages when they are able to take on responsibilities for themselves. Puberty is critically important, when the girl has her first rite of menstruation and the boy his first manhood rite, with teachings shared, taboos untangled, responsibilities understood.

Rites of marriage come in different forms in the tradition, from the relationship which is declared to the community, a handfasting which can be undone by simply returning to the place and walking separately away, to the life-long union blessed with binding vows of love and commitment, the latter usually going hand in hand with a legal ceremony at a registry office.

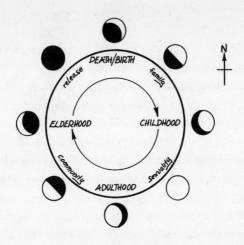

Lunar/life cycle of change

At the farther side of life is the rite of elder, taken when a woman is into her menopause and when a man senses the same shift in his body, the focus moving from the physical to the spiritual. Rites of dying, death and mourning are also practised, working through the processes of healing, honouring and releasing with a profound understanding of the spirit's continued consciousness after leaving the body.

Ceremonies such as baby namings, weddings and funerals can be performed publicly in such a way that family and friends, both Pagan and non-Pagan, can participate without compromising their own religious beliefs.

*What rite of passage in your life do you feel was not properly marked? This may be because it was carried out in a spiritual tradition you did not relate to, or because such a rite was not deemed necessary or relevant. What were the issues which you feel should have been addressed or honoured? Perhaps you would like to put together ideas about how that rite of passage could be performed now.*

**PRINCIPLES OF DRUIDRY**

*If you cannot think of a rite which was not done in your past, consider how you might like to mark a changing point now or in the future.*

## RITES OF INITIATION

Rites of passage take place all through the journey into the tradition: the process of becoming a Druid is a lifelong experience. There is no hierarchy of initiatory grades which one can or must pass through in order to increase one's status or access to teachings. There is no end point.

Pledging with sincerity a personal commitment to the land, to the tradition, to one's ancestry is a profound step which in itself takes the individual through gateways into new spiritual perspectives. Many Groves and Orders offer a rite of initiation that marks the step into that group, this often being woven together with a personal commitment to the journey, a dedication to change and awaken.

On a deeper level, initiation happens as a result of having passed through doorways which activate a significant shift in consciousness. These doorways are often more like long dark tunnels of the subconscious, or veils in the soul's perception, which act as barriers, holding us in a world that we know while constraining our abilities to reach higher potentials. Walking through these boundaries often requires breaking through intense fear. The rite of initiation will then follow the experience, as an acknowledgement and thanksgiving to the forces who have guided us.

As with all rites of passage, initiations may be done both privately, between an individual, her guides, gods and ancestors and the spirits of the land, or with her Druid teacher, or more publicly, witnessed by a Grove or the wider community. Each is considered equally valid.

# THREE FACETS

T he number three was important to our Celtic ancestors. The stability of a trinity is innately satisfying and threes can be found everywhere.

The philosophy of Druidry is built on reverence for the Earth, the ancestors and the gods. Both medieval texts and modern practice focus on the land, the seas and the skies. The bond of male and female, which brings of itself the child, is honoured, as is the play between the head, heart and soul.

Both Irish and Welsh medieval literature contain Triads, threefold mnemonic statements used to remember stories, myths, law codes, regal duties, and so on, many of which have been lost. Iolo Morgannwg added his own, thick with his Druidic philosophy.

Triskal

Spiral

*Awen*

The triskal and triple spiral occur frequently in Celtic design, emphasizing the flow of life energy in the sunwise direction, and the symbol of *awen* is perhaps the most poignant image of triplicity. There are many layers of meaning to this sign, which holds within it the importance of three: the dots are the positions of the sun's rising at the Winter Solstice (SE), the equinoxes (E) and the Summer Solstice (NE). The lines or rays flow out from the sun's light, encouraging life, giving inspiration.

## THREE DROPS OF AWEN

The notion of threes is a key in the stories which for many embody the spirit of *awen* and of Druidry. In the Irish tale of Finn mac Cumaill, the young Finn comes across an old sage who, having spent seven years on the banks of the River Boyne watching its sacred waters, has just managed to catch the Salmon of Wisdom. Finn is happy to build a fire and cook the salmon for the old man but, in checking whether it is done by pinching the flesh, he burns his thumb, which instinctively he puts into his mouth to soothe – and is filled with all the wisdom himself.

The action of sucking his thumb, expressing the innocence of a child and, in doing so, gaining the freedom of perfect knowledge together with the exhilaration of awe at the beauty of the world, is also relayed in the British tale of Cerridwen.

This relates how the dark goddess Cerridwen has given birth to a son who is so dreadfully ugly that she decides to concoct for him a brew which will endow him with perfect wisdom, so that his knowledge might present opportunities that would otherwise be closed to him. As she goes about her task, she sets a young lad called Gwion Bach (meaning 'Little Innocent') to stir the cauldron for the year and the day it will take to perfect. At the last moment, the bubbling brew spits three scalding drops onto the boy's thumb, which he instantly puts into his mouth to ease the pain. In those three drops are held the entire worth of the brew and Gwion is transformed with all that was meant for the goddess' son. After the inevitable tussle with the furious goddess he emerges as the legendary Bard Taliesin.

The cauldron of Cerridwen is one of many in the myths, each holding some divine gift: nourishment, rebirth, abundance, courage, knowledge. The journey that is Druidry is the search for this sacred vessel, the motivation to continue is the thirst to drink from it, to receive the *awen*. Yet the myths imply that this is a search which can be satisfied and concluded, while in reality it is a journey which takes lifetimes, never truly ending, as we inch nearer those sources of inspiration, finding ways in which the flow of divine energy can move through body and soul unhindered, being enriched and not diminished by our experience, and then released, expressed with perfect grace.

While inspiration for most comes in a flash, out of the blue and out of our control, for the Druid this is not sufficient. As she journeys she learns how to access it, flow with it and use it with respect, gradually reaching deeper, higher and brighter.

We each find the exquisite gift of *awen* in unique areas, and in the same way we each use it differently. For some it is poured out as poetry, song or stories, while others use art, dance, relationships, gardening, parenting or politics as media for expressing the divine energy they have received.

*This journey with no clear end also has no clear beginning. The start is marked only by our intention to understand more fully what it is that fuels us.*

*What inspires you, filling you, even if momentarily, with calm, exhilaration and freedom, soul deep? It may be visual, auditory, sensual: a sunset over the ocean, the sound of doves, Mozart, the Ramones, the touch of loving intimacy, ideas, colours, laughter ... Become aware of what fires you. Check that it is positive and in tune with your well-being and that of your environment.*

*Now, taking some time to yourself undisturbed, work with this source of inspiration. Allow yourself to dive into it, surrendering to the flow of its energy. Journey into that place again and again, reaching deeper, breathing in more of its beauty. Let it fill you with energy and, when you return to your normal consciousness, make offerings of thanks.*

*Not only do your offerings honour the forces that touch you with their gifts of vision and strength, but in giving something in return you allow yourself more fully to accept those gifts you have been given.*

# THREE CRAFTS

The drops which Gwion Bach sucked off his scalded thumb imbued him with three gifts: poetry, prophecy and shapeshifting. These skills are key elements in Druidry and explain the different facets within the tradition.

In the Classical texts it becomes clear that Druidry was made up of layers. There were Bards, referred to as *bardoi*; Ovates, called *vates* and perhaps *euhages*; Druids, known as *druides* and also *semnotheoi* (which translates from the Greek as 'reverend gods') and *gutuartri* (with a possible meaning of 'father of invocation'). It was the Stoic philosopher Poseidonios who, in the first century BCE, mentions *bardoi*, *vates* and *druides* together, and these three groups are those which are most widespread in the modern tradition.

It is understood, although nowhere distinctly stated, that the novice began training as a Bard and progressed through the Ovate stage to become a Druid, and many courses of study today focus on each in turn. In some Orders they are called grades, while others call them Groves, levels or crafts. The idea of any hierarchy existing between the levels is avoided, with emphasis being placed on the importance of each of the three roles. There is no dishonour attached to a person who decides to remain within any one in order to perfect the expression of his *awen* through the skills that craft teaches.

## BARDS

The Bards of ancient Britain and Ireland were the poets and singers of the tradition. It was their task, through their dozen years of training, to augment their memory skills sufficiently to carry in their minds some 350 stories, numerous poems, the craft of ogham, the laws of grammar, the laws of their tribes, genealogies and histories, and the myths and lore of the landscape and its sacred sites. They were the bearers of the (oral) tradition, the keepers of the past. Their role was both to affirm and inform the identity of the people and the rights of those people to the land on which they depended.

The Bards offered a source of stability in a world where the immediate future was less certain than it is today. They gave the people their foundation, their roots, and fed those roots with stories of bloody and magical glory, of heroic courage and total devotion, and in doing so they encouraged the people to stretch further towards their potential.

A critical part of their task was to deepen and enrich the connection between the people and the gods of the land. Stories were told of the bond of kings to the goddess of the land, of their successes when the goddess was content and gave abundance, and of the times when the kings failed and the people were scorned by the goddess whose body nourished their land, bringing starvation and war. And through these tales were explained the laws of nature, with warnings woven in to be heeded by kings and priests and those who worked the soil.

There was, and remains still, a sense that the stories were – and are – told not only for the benefit of the tribes, but also for the spirits of the land, as if in their retelling the Bard is practising a sacred art of awakening, enchanting and honouring the spirits of each hill, each lake and tree, each ocean wave and lunar tide. With the music of his words he honours each creature through its deity or collective consciousness. With each nod of intention, each tear and laugh evoked, he honours the ancestors and all humanity. In doing so, and only by doing so, will the spirits and elemental forces continue their task of constantly recreating the world within which we live.

So the Bard was not a simple storyteller, but an acknowledged magician of words.

Many Bardic colleges in these islands were overwhelmed by Roman culture, while others were reprogrammed by Christianity. Yet when the Druids were suppressed because of their political status, the Bards were able to adapt their craft to survive within the different cultural climate.

How the colleges worked is not entirely clear. The use of sensory deprivation is well documented, forcing the Bard to face the single point of stimulus within himself that would crack open into his poem. There is some suggestion that the colleges were only used during spring and autumn; during the summer and winter months the Bards would travel with their teacher to the courts of the land, learning the implementation of their craft.

In early medieval Irish texts *filidh* are mentioned, a *fili* originally meaning a 'seer' but more commonly understood to be a poet. While in Ireland Bards had enjoyed high status in society, by the sixth to eighth century CE the term had slipped to refer to no more than a wandering minstrel, with the word *filidh* replacing it to describe the traditional educated and aristocratic poets and satirists still called Bards in Britain. When the Irish tradition was given a burst of reconstructive energy inspired by the threat of English (Norman) culture in the twelfth century, a *fili* once more became synonymous for a Bard.

The Irish texts talk of a Bard carrying a branch adorned with bells of bronze, silver or gold, the metal declaring his rank or status. This Branch of Peace would be shaken as the Bard prepared to recite, silencing those gathered and calling upon the ancestors and spirits to attend and inspire the recitation.

The Bard's power of language, spoken or sung, was the measure of his talent and he would hone his craft to a point where he was a master of emotion and human desire. He could augment the standing of an individual with eulogies, increasing or assuring a person's status in society. He could deflate or destroy by satire, causing an individual irreparably to reveal his own weakness. It was said that through satire a Bard could cause a person's face to break out in blemishes.

He could invoke the gods of the land, of love and war.

The modern Bard is no less concerned with the use of language, though this has now broadened to include the language of music, sound, colour and movement. Skills of poetry are still greatly honoured, through an understanding that poetry uniquely weaves the left (linear) and right (spatial) sides of the brain. Through his words the Bard shifts the emotions of those gathered to hear, shifts their perceptions of reality, their concepts of boundaries and potentials. Through his own *awen*, he uses his craft in order to inspire others.

While there are few female Bards in the documented history of the tradition, in modern Druidry there are equal numbers of men and women learning the craft, all expressing the *awen* in their own way.

The creativity of the Bard stems from his ability to listen. He has been attuning his ability to access his inspiration, by listening, by opening himself to ideas and relaxing to receive the divine energy that inspirits him. By continuing to listen to the worlds around him, he sharpens his ability to express what he has been given, releasing it into the worlds with honour, respect and the power to evoke change.

Often that change is focused on the human soul, with the source of inspiration coming from the beauty and the power of the land. However, many Bards work to inspire the land, to encourage its own processes to adapt and strengthen itself despite the abuse of mankind, enchanting the spirit folk who have fled or flinched from the destruction of the environment to return and dance their sacred dance, recreating the beauty of the wild and the joy of fertility.

Each hill, each stream, woodland and moor, each circle of stones and sacred spring, each place of potent energy, has its own stories, myths, songs and poetry. The modern Bard will use archaeology, medieval literature and more recent folklore to find these ancestral stories which marry us and our communities to the land, but more often than not he will use no second-hand evidence. The Bards' craft teaches them to listen to the Earth, to the stones, to the water and the wind, and hear the voices that sing within them.

Many Bards spend time listening to the other worlds at places known to contain high energy, where the spirits of the Earth, deities and faery folk are more easily heard. Some choose the wilderness, where evidence of humanity is scarce. Others choose ancient sacred sites, barrows, circles and mounds. Sacred mounds such as the Hill of Tara in Ireland and Silbury Hill in Wiltshire are still sources of much inspiration.

The ancient mounds where kings were inaugurated and tribes gathered together for important occasions were called in Welsh *gorsedd* mounds, *gorsedd* meaning 'high seat'. Nowadays a *gorsedd* is more often translated as the gathering and not the mound itself, in particular a gathering of Bards.

Nowadays, when an individual begins training in the Bardic craft, he first studies the nature and qualities of Earth energies and elemental forces, learning to understand the world around him. The focus is powerfully on the spirits of place, so the Bard will be able to relate what is found and to adapt his work to attune with it, expressing the harmony of the web of connectedness, singing the songs of the land, giving voice to the spirits.

During or after every Druidic ceremony, within the celebration, there is time for these songs, poems and stories, this music and dance to be shared in the eisteddfod. There are occasions when such an event is competitive, with Bards vying with each other to take the Chair of a particular *gorsedd*. This happens in the *gorseddau* of Wales and Cornwall, with equivalent competitions in Ireland and Scotland, and increasingly such events are being organized with substantial support around England.

*How well do you listen? The Bard can touch with his fingers, feet or eyes, and hear. What do you hear as you walk, touching the Earth with your footsteps? What do you hear, with your fingers, in the walls of your home, in a seashell or stone? What do you hear when you look out over your environment?*

## OVATES

The Bardic craft is concerned with that drop of scalding *awen* from the cauldron of inspiration which gives us poetry. The Ovate's drop offers the gift of prophecy.

While the Bard develops his ability to listen to the worlds that surround him, both manifest and spirit, in order to retell what he hears, the ability of the Ovate is in vision and interaction. The Ovate not only hears the voices of those in the spirit worlds and those that inspirit our shared reality of leaf and paw, mud and star, but also converses with the spirits. And in his ability to enter into dialogue with those spirits that create the worlds through which we walk, he has the opportunity to discover what is being made, why and how, to look into the potential of the future and the patterns of the past, and to bring that information back into mundane reality.

The spirits with which the Ovate interacts are not only those of the environment, the trees and streams – the Ovate hones his gift of vision to see and communicate with the spirit of those creatures who live around him, the animals of land, sea and sky, and his fellow human beings. Learning more of his own spirit energy and the spirit powers around him, by making offerings and petitions, with knowledge gleaned, he effects

change in the spirit web and guides through connectedness to health and well-being.

In the same way that not all Bards begin as or become unnervingly good poets, so the level of psychic vision or clairvoyance varies in the Ovate practitioner. For some the vision is profoundly shamanic and the Ovate will interact with exquisite sensitivity with the worlds beyond. There are also Ovates whose sight is so deeply grounded in the simplicity of reality that they are able to access the information they need where others are befuddled by the clutter of distraction.

Though training varies within the tradition, for many the work of the Ovate begins by learning tools of communication, while simultaneously increasing awareness of his own sensitivity, of the dozens of 'eyes' which cover our bodies, from the back of our heads to our hands and feet, and learning how to use these consciously to see in many worlds.

As a healer and seer, an Ovate will use many forms of divination. Some use runes, tarot or other decks of cards, such as the Druid Animal Oracle and the Celtic Tree Oracle (details of which can be found in Chapter Nine). More traditional Ovates will use Ogham staves, reading the threads of connections, past, present and future, in the qualities of the trees. Many use no physical aid other than the world around them, reading messages in cloud formations, in the flight of birds, in spiders' webs and hedgerow plants. While our ancestors in the tradition, as in most spiritual practices of the time, used animal sacrifice and the patterns of entrails in order to know the will of the gods, the Ovate now – understanding that all creation has its own spirit force and therefore holds within it the essential wisdom of nature – will read the signs given by and through the *living* world. Some will simply ask and be given the answer by spirit guides and teachers, be they dryadic or devic, of animal or human form, or indeed divine.

The very word 'divination' speaks of the way in which the Ovate seeks his *awen*, reaching to touch the gods and through that communion be filled with divine inspiration, his vision and communication clear and sure, both between himself and the spirit world and between himself and those he is working for in the mundane world. So his *awen* flows, clear bright energy of healing.

There is little evidence of what position *vates* held 2,000 years ago, and prior to that it is likely that the role of the Ovate was blended with that of the Druid, as priest and physician. When the Roman culture became politically dominant, while the Bards survived and Druids were suppressed into secrecy, the Ovates, as healers and seers, slipped into the background, becoming the wise folk of communities, the herbalists and magicians.

They remained elusive; there is no mention of Ovates in the medieval literature, though the Welsh word *ofydd* is mentioned, translating as 'philosopher', and the Classical texts most often describe the *vates* as 'natural philosophers'. In Ireland, the word *fathi*, derived from *vates*, means 'prophets' or 'seers', though there is no direct evidence that these were a specific section within the educated classes of society; in the medieval literature prophecies are attributed to Druids, *filidh* or Christian monks.

There is little to tell us then who the Ovates were. But if we cast our imagination back to Iron Age Europe, the priest working in the Ovate role would have been a source of great security through the hardest moments of life, taking people through their greatest fears, guiding them with his profound understanding of the natural world. He would have brought women through childbirth with herbs and incantations, and held people through sickness, through insanity and through crises blamed on the spirit worlds. He would have ushered them into death. We know that the power of these priests was strong, if

only through the comments made by Classical writers on the way in which the Celtic people lived and died without fear of death, assured that they would live again.

The modern Ovate, too, works with these mysteries of time and the cycles of life. His focus is on the nature of life and death, on the healing powers of release within life and at its end, and within the nourishing darkness of the cauldron of rebirth: the womb. As he calls through the mists to the ancestral spirits, he is aware of the current of life, from spiritual wisdom to genetic inheritance, that flows from those souls through us and into our descendants. As he honours the flow, on every level he prepares the way for creation, for the beauty of birth.

*Connecting with your source of inspiration, if possible outside, allow a question to arise until you have it clear your mind.*

*Without losing the energy, remaining open and relaxed, look around you, letting some aspect of your environment draw your attention. What does it tell you, in its pattern, that answers your question?*

## DRUIDS

First learning to listen, the Bard extends his powers to hear the worlds of spirit and express them perfectly through his own craft. The Ovate extends further, to see and interact with spirit, allowing the *awen* to flow through his soul as vision and healing. The Druid goes further still: he walks into the otherworlds.

The third drop of *awen* which landed on Gwion's thumb conferred the gift of shapeshifting: the ability to leave one's normal form and the mentality to slide into another, to perceive the world from that alternate state and either to respond from there or bring information back and then take appropriate action.

So the Druid walks between worlds, between forms, and acts as a bridge linking realities.

With these skills, the Druid of two millennia past was the peace-maker, the judicial authority, the principal source of learning, the official in all matters of religion, ceremony and etiquette. In a widely uneducated society, Druids were the learned few. They created and maintained the social structure of their day, to such an extent that, despite the shifting tides of peoples and influences across our nations, it is easy to imagine how much of modern society is based on that distant Druidic framework.

It was said by Classical writers to have taken up to 20 years to become a Druid, though as the Druids measured their calendar in lunar cycles, it is possible that the time may have accorded with the lunar span of 19 years.

Through much of the Classical literature Druids are acknowledged as profound philosophers. This reputation was widely known: Clement of Alexandria even suggested that the study of philosophy itself had its origin amongst the Celtic people. Though the Druids' spiritual doctrine was retained in memory as an oral tradition, being kept both sacred and exclusive to initiates in that way, it was not as if they were isolated from the development of thought across the rest of Europe and Asia. They used Greek letters for all matters needing literacy and were highly numerate, reportedly using Pythagorean principles, with which they developed their knowledge of astronomy and astrology. It is recorded that Druids knew of mountains on the moon, and the size and shape of the Earth. And as the holders of knowledge, they controlled the education of their society.

In terms of science, the calculations that gave prediction and understanding about natural phenomena also gave power to the Druids, as did their knowledge of the Earth's resources. Within Bronze and Iron Age Europe the art of metalworking was critical to a community's strength and safety; in the main this is what gave the Celtic people their cultural advantage. A specialist group of Druids, alchemists called the Pheryllt, mythically based in the town of Emrys in the mountains of north Wales, were said to be responsible for developments in smithcraft.

Druids also held power in matters of law, acting as judge and jury in disputes within the community. Able to listen and see beyond what was superficially presented, working within their own complex legal system, they would settle arguments and make decisions to resolve crises. We may presume that such decisions were taken in consultation with the gods, the spirits of the land and the ancestors, for if the wrong decision were made the spirits would be angered and chaos ensue. As well, the Druid dealt with criminals and set punishments, Classical texts stating this to be especially true in the case of murderers. So the Druids held power over the lives of all in the community and could effectively shame a wrongdoer into the position of an outcast, an untouchable, by banning the individual from attending rites of sacrifice. This was understood to be the 'heaviest penalty' – within a cultural belief of reincarnation, capital punishment was understood to be a significantly easier fate.

The Druids' involvement in human sacrifice remains an awkward issue. Druids were the theologians of their society, orchestrating and overseeing every rite and celebration, and offerings made to the gods and the spirits of the land changed over time. One of the complaints levelled against the Druids of Gaul by the Romans was their use of human sacrifice, be it by impaling, hanging, burning, drowning or eviscerating. There are also references to human sacrifice as a form of divination, victims being disembowelled and omens read in their death throes. It is tempting to want our spiritual ancestors to be less bloody, yet we know that before the Romans stopped the practice Celtic warriors took the heads of their enemies as trophies. It is an expression of the era: Vercingetorix, the leader of the Gallic rebellion, was ritually killed in Rome as part of Caesar's triumph in 45 BCE, despite Caesar being one of the writers who most vigorously condemns the Celts for practising human sacrifice.

As soon as the Romans took over they outlawed the practice and, though archaeological evidence is somewhat lacking, we can assume that it ceased by the end of the first century CE in Britain and Gaul, though it may have survived a little longer in Ireland and Scotland.

The Druids' use of animal sacrifice was not a problem for the Pagan Romans, who practised it themselves. When Christianity spread through Europe, practices did change, though slowly. Giraldus Cambrensis refers to horse sacrifice in Ireland being a part of the inauguration rite of kings as late as the twelfth century, while folklore tells of animals sacrificed well into the last century, though these were offerings made by farmers, not Druids.

With power over religious practice, education and law, the areas of trade and no doubt marriage and other contracts were also under the Druids' control. They were advisors to the tribal kings, defined protocol and taught the heirs. The Druid in modern society has, needless to say, none of the political power of his spiritual ancestors and on the whole he would not want it. Yet there are many underlying aspects of practice which are still present today.

The role of the Druid is still based on the ability to work as a bridge and the training he undertakes for this role is focused on increasing his abilities to empathize and shapeshift, walking deeper into other worlds and understanding the nature of different realities and illusions.

The realities which the Druid brings together are many and varied, and depend upon the special knowledge and interest of

the individual. Some Druids teach, passing on their spiritual and philosophical heritage and bridging gaps in understanding, either working closely with a few apprentices or teaching many students, if less directly and intensely. There are a number who work as teachers in general education, sharing their enthusiasm for learning and their special inspiration with the children of our society.

Others work as counsellors and guides, in law, business or government, or as Druids in their community, resolving conflicts and creating bridges where communication has broken down in personal relationships or between organizations. Bridges may be forged between the sexes, between cultures and religions or in any area affected by a chasm of separation.

The modern Druid might also work as a priest to his community. With the clear premise that Druid priests do not present themselves as the only possible medium between the gods and the people, he will act as a facilitator of ceremony where every person can be as deeply involved as they would wish to be. For those who cannot yet themselves access the realms of the gods or the power of *awen*, the priest offers an open door, while for those who can experience the beauty and exhilaration themselves he merely guides the form of the communal rite. The Druid priest or priestess also performs rites of passage, enabling individuals to cross into new areas of their lives, including those spiritual rites of passage that are levels of initiation.

Druids who work shamanically will often work for their community or for the land as a bridge between the worlds. Walking through the spirit planes, the Druid can make changes closer to the source energy, more precisely moving aspects within the pattern of creation. As a shapeshifter, the Druid can bridge the separation between species, between souls, guiding us to a world of tolerance and harmony.

*In what way do you naturally work as a Druid? Think of a conflict in your world, perhaps a personal relationship, a misunderstanding, and, connecting again with your source of inspiration, work on bridging the gap, healing the problem, giving thanks to your inspirers.*

8

# GUIDES, GUARDIANS AND GODS

We have looked into the origins of the tradition and the importance of inspiration, how it shapes and colours the variations in Druidry. We have also looked at ritual concepts which create a framework within which Druidry is practised, such as the sacred circle which is both a sanctuary for inner growth and healing and a temple to the power and beauty of nature. We have looked at the Druid's perception of the changing tides and the way in which these cycles offer potential for transformation and regeneration through a sensitivity to fertility, growth, decay and rebirth, within the seasons of our climate and the processes of the human soul. We have seen how these cycles are honoured and celebrated. Turning again to inspiration, we have viewed the ways in which it is expressed within the spirit of Druidry, through the three crafts of the tradition.

*Before taking the final step in this book, weigh up the information you have gleaned, both through these words and through the images and emotions they have evoked.*

*How do you now relate to what were suggested as the key principles of Druidry: honouring the Earth and the ancestors, through the search for inspiration? How do the tenets of equality and tolerance fit in?*

Before long, anyone studying the faith with dedication will feel the presence of ancestral Druids, clarifying her vision in a way which increases awareness, revealing how it is the *practice* of Druid ritual and perception that is our most potent teacher. With clearer sight, the sacred circle becomes a mentor in itself, painted with the images and colours of our subconscious and displaying its web of internal paths. Awareness of the changing cycles of time also acts as a guide, offering discipline and wisdom to our developing practice.

With no scripture to refer to, Druids also learn to communicate, in words or feelings, with the spirits of nature, the faeryfolk and devas of the plants of our local environment, the dryads and boggarts of woodlands and marshes, and these too guide us, revealing not simply their own lore and power but taking us deeper into ours. In accessing abilities to empathize with animals, feathered and furry, the swimmers and sliders, perhaps even to shapeshift, the Druid learns tough and important lessons in equality and tolerance, in what is appropriate action, in when to take responsibility, when to bite down and when to let go.

These spirits of nature hold and enrich our inner groves and our outer worlds. They are the willow at the garden gate, the beeches of the forest temple, the herbs we infuse for teas that wake and soothe us. They are the pets that welcome us, the wild creatures of land and seas, the animals that roam our inner worlds. They are the spirits that offer us the food we need, teaching us humility, dependency and respect.

Yet more powerful are the elementals, the spirits of the winds, rains, rivers, oceans, rocks and storms, fires and lightning. These too teach us, as do the spirits of place, the spirit guardians that hold the energy of mountains, moors, woodlands and waterfalls, as well as our tended groves and gardens.

Their very being reveals to us areas of our psyche, our emotional and instinctual bodies, our beliefs and expectations, that would otherwise be veiled in the subconscious, and by relating to them more closely, by moving deeper into their powers, consciously we heal and regenerate, refining the many layers of our body and soul.

Together with our ancestors, these spirit beings are honoured in ritual practice and invited to witness, bless, protect and inspire each ceremony, which in itself is a celebration of awe and thanksgiving for the power those spirits bring to our worlds. Each is potentially a source of that perfect inspiration at the heart of Druidry.

Indeed, some look no further. Before them, around them, within them are all the powers of nature, of creation and destruction, of brilliance and inundation, of clarity and chaos, the manifest and the potential. This, surely, is sufficient, if the goal of the journey is the exquisite joy of accessing the highest inspiration and its perfect expression through beauty, power and knowing. All the powers of nature are more than enough.

But others look beyond – to the realms of the gods.

## WHAT ARE GODS?

Whether gods are merely archetypes, particular tones of life energy, or real entities, independent of the human race, brings us back not to a debate but simply to restate that both these attitudes are found amongst modern Druids. Either way, the notion of deity describes a source of power.

Deities can indeed be purely elemental forces and powers of nature. Here we are simply referring to the vibrational 'intelligence' of hills, lakes and hurricanes as 'gods' instead of 'spirits'. At some point during our evolution our vision of these energies developed into form. The more powerful spirits became deities, some taking on animal characteristics, some blending animal with human and others becoming fully human images. None the less, the powers, energies, emotions, motivations of these gods remained entirely non-human.

There are also gods who relate more closely to the human psyche than the natural world outside it. These too are forces of guidance, strength, validation and power, and are usually associated with our ancestors. More often than not, in their dealings with the human race they are seen in human form and the teachings they offer typically emphasize those of the ancestors: they are the gods of our ancestors. Reverence for these gods strengthens the continuity and development of our bloodline and our tradition.

Some understand these gods to have been spirits of place that resided in the lands where our ancestors settled. Through perhaps generations of interaction, the tribal connection with those spirits became so strong that when the people moved on they took with them their reverence for those divine guiding spirits. The spirits then offered the tribe the *qualities* which had been embodied in the land they left, be it strength, beauty, intelligence, harmony, fluidity, warmth, or whatever. They became guardians of the tribe, or of individual members of the tribe.

Some would dispute this idea and declare the gods of love and war, of communication and agriculture, metalcraft, healing, sacrifice, birth, death, justice and the rest, to be superbeings of worlds beyond those we can perceive, beings who, when adequately tempted to give us their attention, will move through the gateways that divide our worlds and breathe their energy into our work – for a fee. They are distinctly not human, though, and do not guide from ethical or moral frameworks that automatically work for our society here and now; the gods of the natural world work within the principles of natural law,

tooth and claw, but the gods of worlds beyond have their own laws entirely.

Some gods are seen simply as mythical heroes. Earlier we saw how Bards were expected to recite genealogies that traced the bloodline from their king back to these ancient figures. Maybe they were people who, by some extraordinary act, were magnified to the status of deity. Having played a key role in the history of their people, they were put on a par with the guardian spirits of the land. Alternatively, they may have been deities diminished to mythical human status by an invading culture and the deities they brought with them.

## THE GODS OF OUR ANCESTORS

Enough evidence remains to give us a fairly clear picture of the deities of these islands between the middle of the first millennium BCE and the medieval era, though how much Druids themselves had to do with these gods we cannot be sure. Most probably, while people had their own individual deities, of their family, hearth, local environment, their craft and ancestors, all of whom would be reverenced with prayers, offerings and small-scale sacrifice, Druids would have been summoned for anything more important.

Working with spirit energies and the mysteries of natural law, the Druid would invoke both her own divine allies and the gods of those she was working for to guide and vitalize the work. There appears, however, to have been a reluctance to mention the gods by name. Perhaps this was simply because the vast majority of gods were so localized. The Celtic oath first recorded in Classical texts and still used in Ireland a thousand years later stated simply, 'I swear by the gods my people swear by.'

Whether Druids had their own pantheon as well is debatable. There are a small number of gods with similar names across

Europe, implying a wider base for their religious practice, Druids having total freedom to move across tribal boundaries. Most of these names, however, are simply descriptives that would have been important to any Pagan peoples, translating into words such as 'mother', 'young one', 'mist', 'shining', 'smith', and the like.

Archaeology has revealed iconography from Bronze and Iron Age Europe, particularly southern Britain and France, which suggests a focus on deities of the sun, thunder, water, hunting and battle, and a common theme of a triple goddess. The Celtic culture was widely non-literate and it was not until the Roman invasion that altars and statues started bearing names. Yet still such an enormous number of deities are represented that any attempt to reconstruct a religious system becomes quickly tangled, taking us back to the understanding that deity was more about the spirit of place than some wider social order.

One of the few Classical writers who mentions the gods of Celtic culture was Caesar and even then he refers to them by what he considers their Roman names. Mercury, he states, was the favourite deity amongst the Gallic people, being the god of trade, travel and skill, followed by Apollo, Mars, Jupiter and Minerva.

## THE GODS OF MODERN DRUIDS

With local gods and spirit guardians overwhelmingly the most common form of deity with our ancestors, the deities of the local environment are still the principal focus of devotions amongst dedicated Druids today.

However, many look back to find the gods of the old tribes too and medieval literature offers information about many of these deities, both the spirits of place and the mythical heroes. It is difficult to correlate the mythology in the literature with

the archaeological finds and the Classical evidence, however, indicating again the importance of local gods. This also reveals the problems of working with texts so profoundly influenced by other cultures, not least the Christian. None the less, Druids who now wish to work with Celtic gods other than their local spirits of place look to texts such as the Welsh *Mabinogion* and the Irish *Tain* and *Lebor Gabala Erinn* ('The Book of Invasions').

There are many books on the market now which list the gods of the Celtic pantheons and give descriptions of their characteristics, attributes and relationships. Reading the old texts will reveal their stories. Here I offer only a brief outline, with recommendations for further reading in Chapter Nine.

## BRITISH GODS

Welsh literature tells of old British gods disguised as an intriguing collection of proud kings, brave knights and beguiling ladies. They are rulers of the land and the underworld, spirits of the earth and waters. As most of the tales were written down by Christian monks, we can be sure that much of the clarity and power of the gods has been diminished, but with some work there can be found sufficient gateways for the Druid now to reach these gods once again.

The earlier figures are divided into the Children of Don and the Children of Lyr, and some speculate that these were the gods of the skies and those of the underworld, but it is more likely that they were simply of different (though overlapping) regions and times.

Of the key figures, one of the most commonly invoked in modern Druidry is Arianrhod, daughter of the mother goddess Don and of Beli Mawr, from whom all medieval dynasties claim descent. She is a goddess of the stars, in particular the constellation Corona Borealis, her Caer (castle) Arianrhod. She is called the Lady of the Silver Wheel, and rules over birth and initiation. Two of her brothers are Govannon, the smith god, and the god of agriculture, Amaethon.

Gwyddion is both another brother and also Arianrhod's lover. He is a lord of the skies – the Milky Way is Caer Gwyddion – and a god of words, a Bard. They have three sons, the first being Lleu Llaw Gyffes, possibly one of the gods Caesar called Mercury. 'Lleu of the Skilful Hand' is a god of many skills and a favourite amongst modern Druids. Cursed by Arianrhod never to wed a human woman, he marries the beautiful Blodeuwedd, who was created by his uncles out of flowers, and who deceives him. Another of Arianrhod's sons, Dylan, god of the waves, is killed by her brother Govannon.

Of the Children of Lyr, Manawyddan, another god of the sea, was married to Rhiannon, the horse goddess and so also a goddess of the land. Her first husband was Pwyll, Prince of Dyfed and a lord of Annwn, the underworld. The god of the underworld is Arawn, a hunter of souls who rides his grey horse through the dusk with his pack of white hounds with alarming red ears.

Bran is a guardian of the land and a god of war, whose head was said to be buried on the White Mount of London, where the Tower of London now stands, protecting Britain from invaders. His sister, Branwen, is a goddess of love and death.

Cerridwen, holder of the cauldron of inspiration and rebirth, is a dark mother goddess and possibly the most important goddess in the Welsh medieval literature, referred to countless times in the poetry of the Bards and highly revered by modern Druids.

## THE IRISH GODS

The Irish deities have a different texture. Less influenced by Christianity, their stories are fuller and give a clearer history of the island, however mythological that may be. Where the stories of Britain and Ireland overlap we find battles between

the two, and some of the gods are similar, possibly due to common influences but also reflecting immigrations from Ireland into Wales after the Roman withdrawal.

Many of the Irish gods now revered within Druidry are of the Tuatha de Danaan, the Children of Danu, a superhuman race who at Beltane in some year of prehistory conquered the Fir Bolg and took the island as their own. When later they themselves were overwhelmed it is said that the Tuatha disappeared into the sacred hills of the Earth where they became the faeryfolk, the Sidhe. Others submerged beneath the waves, heading for the otherworlds of the western horizon.

Dagda is the father god, known as the Good God and Lord of Knowledge. He is coarser than the other members of the Tuatha de Danaan, implying that his 'father' status comes from his being an older god adopted into the pantheon. Dressed as a peasant, pot-bellied and dragging a vast club set on wheels, he is lord of life and death, offering abundance and rebirth from his vast cauldron of plenty. The Dagda is said to have mated at Samhain with the goddess Boann (of the River Boyne) and the Morrigan, a triple goddess of war and death (by the River Unius). Anghus Og, god of love, is a son of the Dagda and Boann.

In many ways similar to the Dagda, yet younger and more refined, with a spear replacing the great wooden club, is Lugh, the 'shining' god, comparable with Lleu Llaw Gyffes. He is grandson of Balor, whose single eye burns with a ray of withering heat. Lugh's son is Cu Chulainn, one of the great mythical heroes of the Irish texts and a guardian of the land.

Danu or Dana is a mother goddess of the land and a river goddess, similar to the British Don. Her name means 'sacred gift' and for some within the tradition it is used in the same way as the Welsh word *awen*, denoting inspirational energy. Some say Danu is also Brighid, a triple goddess of healing, poetry and smithcraft. Brighid is known by many similar names, slipping into Christianity as Saint Bridget, said to be the foster mother of Christ.

Among the other Irish gods, Bile is a god of death, some say husband to Danu. Mannanan Mac Lir is the sea god. Goibh-nui is god of smithcraft and beermaking, similar to the Welsh Govannon. Macha is the wild fertility goddess of Ulster, a warrior and protector of the land.

## OTHER GODS

Not all modern Druids who work with non-local deities honour those of the Irish or British myths. The old Gallic gods are also acknowledged in some parts of the tradition. Esus, whose name means 'lord' or 'master', is said to be god of the sacred oak. Taranis is the god of thunder, a powerfully savage god said to have demanded human sacrifice. Teutates was a tribal god, a god of war whom both the Romans and many modern Pagans connect with Mars. Cernunnos, a horned fertil-ity god of the wildwood, is one of the most popular gods in modern Paganism, while many Druids revere the Saxon gods, such as Woden and Freyja.

As Druids look into their ancestry of blood and spirit, gods creep into their practice from pantheons across the world, as well as those whose culture has spread to these islands. Classical deities, such as Mercury and Minerva, are not uncommonly revered in the tradition now.

In honouring both the spirits and gods of the land beneath our feet, and the gods of our ancestors and of our own soul, those we bring with us to this place, here and now, we find the guiding principles of Druid devotional practice.

An important element in the tradition is the goddess of the land, in particular through her relationship with the king. If the bond between them was strong, the goddess would bless the

land with abundance, but if he dishonoured her she would cause devastation. A king who could not satisfy the goddess of his land was not a strong enough king and would quickly be challenged by one more powerful.

There are many stories in both the Irish and Welsh texts of how the bond between goddess and king was made. The sacred marriage between the land and the king was, in some cases, played out annually on ancient mounds, such as Tara. The Irish word for the marriage in many texts is *feis*, wrongly translated as 'feast' – it comes from *fo-ais*, meaning 'to sleep with'. In the twelfth century Giraldus Cambrensis tells of the public ceremony in Ulster where the king mated with a white mare which was then ritually slaughtered, cut up and boiled. The king bathed in the broth while he and those gathered ate the meat. Whether this actually happened or not, or how common an event it might have been, we cannot know.

The connection between horses and the goddess of the land is common, reminding us that Celtic culture found much of its strength in the use of horses in battle. One of the best known myths is that of Pwyll who, sitting on the mound of Arberth, is captivated by the sight of Rhiannon riding past on her white mare. The ancient chalk figure at Uffington, Wiltshire, is a particularly sacred place for many Druids, its white horse symbolizing the essential power of the land.

## THE CAULDRON AND DAGGER

Few ritual tools, if any, are needed in Druid practice. Many Druids have a chalice for the consecrating water and a censer, of ornate metal or simple stone. A chalice or drinking horn is commonly used for the mead, wine or ale that is shared with the gods and ancestors and all who have gathered for a ceremony. Some have a sacred dish on which offerings are given to the spirits of the dead and the spirits of nature, often a portion of the family meal. The use of altar cloths, candlesticks, drums, musical instruments and other tools is varied and is a non-essential part of an individual's expression of beauty and devotion.

There are two objects, however, which though not obligatory are commonly found, either materially or symbolically, in both Druid ritual and philosophy. These are the sword and the cauldron.

The relevance of these two objects as metalwork is important, reminding us how much the power of ancient Celtic culture was dependent on their ironsmiths. The Pheryllt, those Druid masters of metal, may well have made the innovations that were a source of such strength to the people. To modern Druids, the ore of the earth, liquefied in fire, cooled in water and raised into the air, takes the sword through all four elements in their extreme. In terms of the human psyche, the work takes clarity and knowledge, courage and strength, desire and energy, to come into perfect form, also leading us through the four elements of growth and change, each in its heightened state.

The cauldron, itself formed by the elements, is also a holder of that process, physically and psychologically. For most it is perceived as a feminine tool, the black iron that holds the fluid suggesting the dark womb of a mother goddess, heated over the fires of transformation.

The holy grail which is the source of life, the focus of the most sacred knightly quest in the Arthurian myths, is understood to be another version of this cauldron of the goddess, here refined into something almost intangible, too exquisite and too potent to behold and carrying with and within it, once again, the power of life and death.

It is from the Arthurian myths, those late medieval stories of the ancient British gods disguised, that the sword is brought

into modern Druidry. A symbol of masculine energy, it has been gently refined over the years and shines sharp and clean, hailing light and justice. The wide and rougher dagger that would have been the contemporary of the first strong iron cauldron has connotations of a pure and brutal male force which, for many in the tradition now, is unacceptable. For these Druids, the qualities of Excalibur have taken its place.

In Druid ritual the sword is used, among other things, to call the peace, to cast the circle, for the swearing of oaths, and as a symbol of male deity and the guardianship of the land. The cauldron is more often physically found in Druidic rites that are shamanic or goddess focused, but its imagery is common, as a source of regeneration and a doorway into the soul.

## BEYOND AND WITHIN

It is understood within Druidry that beyond the interaction with spirits of nature and deity is pure life force. Yet because the essence of all existence is spirit, and life force is the energy at the core of each and every spirit, it is by journeying into the essence that we find the universal Oneness of being. For many in Druidry this is simply energy and so far beyond human comprehension that it can only be understood as such. Indeed, to give this force any characteristics at all would be to limit it, to dishonour it: its wholeness must to us remain as perfect mystery.

While some revere this dark unknown and its potential chaos, others in the tradition believe there is an intelligence and a pattern within this essential energy, clues of which can be found in all life. It is only by meditating at this level, by taking the light of consciousness into that darkness, that there is, they maintain, any hope of understanding existence.

The great forger, Iolo Morgannwg, offers us the concept of Circles of Existence. The source of these ideas is unknown, though it is easy to see how Morgannwg could have devised them himself, blending the philosophies of his time. Some within the tradition do use the model, none the less.

In the centre Iolo placed *annwn*, the Celtic underworld, the place of death and transformation within the magical darkness of the cauldron. Taking form, a spirit moves out of *annwn* to journey through the spirals of *abred*, where all creation exists, the elements, the plant realms, the animal worlds and humankind. It is understood that a period well spent in one form will take the soul to another ring of the spiral, to a higher consciousness of life, while abuse of the life force might spin the soul back down into the cauldron of *annwn*, there to be transformed to begin over again. Beyond the spirals of *abred* is the light of *gwynvid*, the realm of those who have broken free, the wise ones and the many gods. Beyond this circle is the perfect mystery of *ceugant*, the place of Oneness.

It is also possible to understand *annwn* to be the infinite darkness of space, the spirals of *abred* being our worlds that spin within it, *gwynvid* the guiding spirit within *abred*, and *ceugant* the spark at the essential still centre.

## PERFECT EXCHANGE

Relationship is the key to the way Druids work with their deities. While there is clear acknowledgement of the gods' power, there is no sense of authority or hierarchy between gods and humankind. Neither are the gods thought of as infallible; after all, it is only humans who work with the ethics of human society and, while the gods can clarify our vision, they may have very different and even unacceptable ideas as to what should happen. Even if we look at a goddess of nature, an Earth goddess, it is clearly understood that her priorities are focused

on her own perpetual regeneration rather than any concept of the survival of the human or any other species.

A Druid will strive to enchant a deity with whom she'd like to work. Giving offerings of reverence to nature and to the ancestors as a whole, she will endeavour to remain open, listening, waiting for a god or goddess to come to her. After that first connection has been made, the process is then about building a strong relationship with that deity, learning through respect to understand the divine power and learning through devotion how it is that she can give to that god of herself.

There is surrender, yet no sense of submission. The Druid will be uncovering too, through a growing clarity and consciousness, what it is that she wants, if her deity can provide that and how she can accept it. It may be protection, love, security, freedom, healing, teaching: all the issues which disintegrate when we are separated from our own power and that of the universal life force, perceiving ourselves to be disconnected from the web of spirit. Thrown into the crises of scarcity because of that separation, we might be needing food, money or just a parking space. But more often than not, within the tradition nothing more specific is requested than simply inspiration. The Druid knows that, with the gift of divine inspiration received, she will have all she needs: the idea or solution and the energy to make it happen.

To fully accept any gift, though, we need to have given sufficiently in return. Our relationships with the gods are built on this need for perfect exchange. We offer of ourselves, both through sacrifice and through joy, giving back to the gods the creativity born of our inspiration. As our offerings are accepted, so we succeed in holding the attention of the deity, thereby nourishing the relationship. And as the relationship develops, the flow of divine energy which we are offered also grows, as do our love and trust, together with our ability to give … and to receive.

# AWEN

Reaching deep into the beauty and power of creation, through the natural world and the ancestors, the Druid offers her prayers of love and respect, opening to receive the flow of divine energy. It is in this practice of pure devotion that she touches and is touched by spirit, and the result is the sharing of energy.

The deep sensuality of that experience is emphasized by the understanding that it is born of the relationship with the spirits of nature, with the spirits of her ancestors and her gods, spirits which are most often resident within or present themselves through the natural world, be it a river or tree, the wind or a sacred mound, a cat or lover. The depth of experience is amplified by the depth of the relationship the Druid has forged with that spirit, offering the opportunity for deeper trust and therefore a more profound intimacy and surrender.

The experience of communion, of sharing energy with spirit, of opening to receive the *awen*, intensifies the Druid's perception and experience of the worlds within which she lives, because of the heightened awareness caused by the increased flow of energy. This in itself opens the mind to different levels of reality, broadening the perception and experience of life as a whole.

Spirit to spirit, consciously we reacknowledge how we are connected, tree to bird to cat to woman to man, through the land, through time, to our ancestors and gods. Consciously, with respect, we allow the perfect fluidity to flow once more, unchecked, revitalizing our souls and all the world.

*After all you have read so far, together with your changing perception and experience of life, do you sense there is a deity with whom you'd like to work? It may be a character from the myths, or guardian spirit or elemental of the natural world. From all you intuit about this god,*

*create an altar to honour it. How does it connect to the land you live in or where you have lived before? How does it connect to your ancestors? Make your offerings every day, gifts of your creativity, your soul and your life, and wait, open to all you would receive. Listen.*

# THE JOURNEY ON ...

**D**ruidry is growing at an extraordinary rate. As a spirituality which offers us ways of reconnecting with the powers of our land and our sacred heritage, offering links to the past and so into the future, it seems to counter the trend of many centuries of a culture which denies us our natural processes of regeneration. By bringing the brilliance of spirit into the physical world, it validates the sensuality of our experience, enabling us to perceive new depths of beauty and strength. Through honouring death, sexuality and change within nature, it offers a deeply affirming philosophy, offering us a freedom with which we ourselves can utilise these processes, and by so doing enjoy the continuous stimulation of renewal.

Its focus on nurturing creativity is based on the premise of celebrating individuality, the uniqueness of each soul's experience and growth. Yet because of this the wider reality of Druidry, as it is expressed through an ever increasing number of Orders and Groves world-wide, is harder and harder to describe.

## GROVES AND ORDERS

It would be impossible to list here all the Orders and Groves that now exist. There are books which attempt to do this, for both historical reasons and to enable networking, but there would not be space in this introductory book.

There are listed here, however, some of the larger and more open Orders. It must be left up to the individual to judge whether any person they meet, associated with these or any other groups, shares their vision of Druidry and is worthy of their attention and resources. The reason for listing the Orders I do is because they are useful for making contacts, whether the seeker is looking for more information, for training or for open celebration that they can attend. By picking up a copy of one of the books which lists more Orders, others can easily be found.

If the training of a Druid used to take some 20 years, it may now seem strange to be offered a course which lasts only a year, or perhaps four. This is done with the clear understanding that the process of becoming a Druid is at least one lifetime's work and during that time a person will work with many teachers, in many different ways. Some Druids teach and learn through the apprenticeship system, while others work within Groves or by correspondence course with tutors.

In the search for a teacher, there must above all be trust. Any sense of superiority is a sign saying 'Back off!' Such a person may be a good teacher, but not for you! Perfect equality and perfect tolerance must be evident in any who teach. Druidry is about perfecting the art of connectedness, relationship, soul to soul, spirit to spirit, and it is through the warmth of interaction that we find our courage for the journey.

These are listed in alphabetical order:

**The British Druid Order** (BDO), run by the founder Philip Shallcrass and myself as joint chiefs, came into being in 1979. It organizes events, workshops, conferences and talks in Britain and around the world, including public and private ritual for rites of passage and the major festivals. It publishes books and periodicals, including *The Druids' Voice*. Contact: BDO, PO Box 29, St Leonards-on-Sea, East Sussex TN37 7YP, UK. The Internet web page is at: http://www.druidorder.demon.co.uk

**The Druid Clan of Dana** is another international Order with many Groves world-wide. It was founded in 1992 by Lawrence and Olivia Durdin-Robertson and operates as a part of the Fellowship of Isis, the largest goddess-centred network in the world. Contact: The FOI, Clonegal Castle, Enniscorthy, Eire.

**The Druid College of Albion** is a gathering of Druids from many Pagan Druid Orders which offers a correspondence course rich in Celtic culture and star lore. Students have a personal tutor to guide them through the training. Contact: BM Stargrove, London WC1N 3XX, UK.

**The Gorsedd of Bards of the Isles of Britain** organize public celebrations at the major festivals at Avebury and other ancient sacred sites in Britain and around the world. Ceremonies are family affairs, open to followers of any tradition, held in the spirit of Druidry and include rites of passage, initiation into the Gorsedd and open eisteddfod. Contact: BDO, PO Box 29, St Leonards-on-Sea, East Sussex TN37 7YP, UK. In America, contact: The Bards of Caer Pugetia, PO Box 9785, Seattle, WA 98109, USA.

**The Henge of Keltria**, one of the larger American Orders, runs a correspondence course with a strong Celtic leaning. There are Groves across the country sharing the ceremonies and teachings of the Order. Contact: Henge of Keltria, PO Box 48369, Minneapolis, MN 55448-0369, USA.

**The Order of Bards, Ovates and Druids** (OBOD) is the largest Order world-wide, led by chosen chief Philip Carr Gomm, many of whose books are listed below. Ross Nichols created the Order in 1964, but after his death in 1975 there was a period of dormancy until Philip, a former student of Nichols, resurrected it in 1988. OBOD runs a correspondence course which runs through the three grades of the tradition, giving a sound and inspiring grounding for any study of Druidry. Students are supported by a tutoring system. There are numerous Groves and groups which meet regularly all around the world, each with its own character and focus. Contact: OBOD, PO Box 1333, Lewes, East Sussex BN7 1DY, UK. Their Internet web page is at: http://www.obod.co.uk

# FURTHER READING

Emma Restall Orr, *Spirits of the Sacred Grove* (Thorsons, 1998): a very personal weave of experiential Druidry and healing philosophy, revealing Druidry in its many colours.

## DRUIDRY

Philip Carr Gomm, *Elements of the Druid Tradition* (Element Books, 1991): a short book doing much the same as this one, only with a different style and focus.

Philip Carr Gomm, *The Druid Way* (Element Books, 1993): a journey through the Sussex countryside, weaving Druid history, philosophy and experience with psychotherapy.

Philip Carr Gomm (Ed.), *The Druid Renaissance* (Thorsons, 1996): a fascinating collection of articles written by prominent members of the Druid community.

Ross Nichols, *The Book of Druidry*, edited by Philip Carr Gomm and John Matthews, (Aquarian, 1990): it is quite a tome but filled with genuine eccentricity and interest.

Philip and Stephanie Carr Gomm, *The Druid Animal Oracle*
(Simon & Schuster, 1995): a divination deck filled with animal
lore and mythology, with illustrations by Bill Worthington
which make it worth its weight in gold.

## MYTHS

Jeffrey Ganz, *The Mabinogion* (Penguin, 1976): one of the best
translations of this key text of Welsh medieval literature.

Jeffrey Ganz, *Early Irish Myths and Sagas* (Penguin, 1981):
equally good on the Irish myths.

Thomas Kinsella, *The Tain* (Oxford University Press, 1970): a
great translation of the Irish epic.

John Matthews, *A Druid Source Book* (Cassell, 1996): featuring
some medieval literature together with a good deal of the
eighteenth-century revival material.

Philip Shallcrass, *The Story of Taliesin* (British Druid Order,
1997): a clear and vibrant, annotated version of this key text.

## HISTORY

Miranda Green, *Exploring the World of the Druids* (Thames and
Hudson, 1997): useful and accessible for history if rather
inaccurate on modern Druidry.

Ronald Hutton, *The Pagan Religions of the Ancient British Isles*
(Blackwell, 1991): one of the best texts on British Pagan
history, if rather academic, blowing out all the invalid
assumptions and the romantic misconceptions.

Ronald Hutton, *Stations of the Sun: A History of the Ritual Year in
Britain* (Oxford University Press, 1996): the only work
available which so comprehensively deals with this issue.

142 Prudence Jones and Nigel Pennick, *A History of Pagan Europe* (Routledge, 1995): a well written and accessible text which covers all of Europe and a must if you can't face Ronald Hutton's *Pagan Religions*.

Anne Ross, *Pagan Celtic Britain* (Routledge, 1967): a classic.

## TREES

Ellen Evert Hopman, *Tree Medicine, Tree Magic* (Phoenix, 1992): an interesting and well crafted book on tree lore and Druid spirituality.

Ellen Evert Hopman, *A Druid's Herbal* (Destiny Books, 1995): as above, on herbs.

Jacqueline Memory Patterson, *Tree Wisdom* (Thorsons, 1997): a beautiful and informative book on trees and Druidry.

Liz and Colin Murray, *The Celtic Tree Oracle* (Rider, 1988): a delightful divination set with useful tree lore.

Nigel Pennick, *The Secret Lore of Runes and Other Ancient Alphabets* (Rider, 1991): runes and ogham and all the rest.

## OTHER ORDERS

Philip Shallcrass, *A Druid Directory* (British Druid Order, 1997): a regularly updated edition listing all the working Druid Orders and Groves in Britain, with many from around the world.

## THE FUTURE

Where Druidry is heading as a spirituality of freedom and creativity, reaching into the indigenous wisdom of these European islands, yet relevant world-wide, is an exciting concept. If you choose to follow its path through time to come, may you be guided well. May your gods be with you!

# INDEX

*Of further interest …*

# SPIRITS OF THE SACRED GROVE
## THE WORLD OF A DRUID PRIESTESS

### EMMA RESTALL ORR

For many, the word Druidry conjures up images of white-robed figures involved in esoteric rituals. But modern Druidy is not wrapped in a veil of secrecy – it is celebrated openly, in the sunlight of the meadow or the shady leafiness of a forest glade. Druids are passionate about the environment, and their worship is above all focused on Nature through the celebration of the changing seasons of the year.

*Spirits of the Sacred Grove* is a very personal journey through the seasons seen through the eyes of a modern female Druid. Emma Restall Orr takes the reader through the cycles of nature, from the chaos of Samhain or Hallowe'en into the dark of winter, through the energy of spring and into the bright summer months – then back through Autumn to Samhain. At the same time she acts as a guide along the paths of the sacred rituals.

This is an accessible and compelling spiritual path that offers enormous potential for personal healing and empowerment.

# THE BOOK OF DRUIDRY

ROSS NICHOLS

The Book of Druidry is a comprehensive study of the Druids, from their earliest history to the present-day renaissance. The book includes an examination of the ideas that shaped the druids – their principal deities, their myths, their wisdom and learning and their social organization. It explores their relationship with Arthur, the Grail and Taliesin, and the mystery of the Druid Egg and the Serpent, and explains the significance of dolmens, barrows and stone circles, in relation to many sacred sites. A selection from the early source texts, and the entire text of the Order's Beltane ritual, complete this extensive volume.

Ross Nichols was the Chosen Chief of the Order of Bards, Ovates and Druids from 1964 to 1975, during which time he worked on this definitive account of the history and practice of Druidry. However, for almost a decade following his sudden death, the book was lost, as indeed were most of the papers and teachings of the Order. Through a series of extraordinary events, both the book and the papers were rediscovered, resulting in the rebirth of the modern Order, and the eventual publication of this volume.

# THE DRUID RENAISSANCE

## EDITED BY PHILIP CARR-GOMM

Drawn together in this collection are contributions from Druid Chiefs from Britain, France and America, together with writers and mystics, healers and psychologists, professors and historians. Expressing the excitement and breadth of the modern Druid Renaissance, this book is a celebration of the flowering of a tradition that is ancient yet ever new.

Philip Carr-Gomm is a psychologist, writer and Chief of the Order of Bards, Ovates and Druids. He is author of *The Elements of the Druid Tradition* and *The Druid Way*, co-author of *The Druid Animal Oracle* and editor of *The Book of Druidry*.

# SOPHIA – GODDESS OF WISDOM
## THE DIVINE FEMININE FROM BLACK GODDESS TO WORLD-SOUL

### CAITLÍN MATTHEWS

*Sophia – Goddess of Wisdom* takes the reader on a journey from pre-Christian spirituality to the present day, seeking out the presence of the Goddess – the divine feminine power of wisdom. Drawing mainly on sources from the Western tradition, the many faces of the Goddess are revealed: she is the primeval Black Goddess of the earth, the Saviour Goddess, the Gnostic Sophia, the World-Soul, the Apocalyptic Virgin, the Mother of God. We see how the foundation mysteries of the Goddess underlie the esoteric currents of orthodox religions, and trace her hermetic presence in Qabala and alchemy through to her emergence in the realms of Goddess religion, feminist theology and the New Age Movement. This definitive work gives Sophia a voice that will be welcomed by all who seek to reaffirm the Goddess as the central pivot of creation and as the giver of practical and spiritual wisdom.

Caitlín Matthews is the author of 26 books on Celtic traditions, practical spirituality and shamanism. She has a busy shamanic practice dedicated to soul-work in Oxford, where she lives with the writer John Matthews.

# LADIES OF THE LAKE

## CAITLÍN AND JOHN MATTHEWS

*Ladies of the Lake* portrays nine of the women in Arthurian legend: Igraine, Guinevere and Morgan, who are Arthur's kindred; Argante, Nimue and Enid, who bring the wisdom of the otherworld; and Kundry, Dindraine and Ragnell, who manifest the compassion of the Grail. These are the Ladies of the Lake in whom the ancient Celtic Goddess is fragmented and reflected. Just as Arthur's Knights assemble about the Round Table to discover their quest, so the Arthurian Ladies gather about the deep waters of the Lake to draw upon their innate gifts. And just as the mysterious element of water permeates all life, so the influence of the Ladies of the Lake permeates the whole Arthurian legend. They are the empowerers, guardians and transformers whose wisdom is still accessible today.

Caitlin and John Matthews are the authors of over 60 books, many of which explore the Arthurian world and the spiritual dimension of the Goddess.

# TREE WISDOM
## THE DEFINITIVE GUIDEBOOK TO THE MYTH, FOLK-LORE AND HEALING POWER OF TREES

### JACQUELINE MEMORY PATERSON

*Tree Wisdom* explores the world of trees through the eyes of the ancients and our eyes of today. Trees existed long before humans and provide a unique holistic insight into our relationship with the land. In this time of increasing ecological awareness trees have become a symbol of our connection with nature.

Concentrating on the indigenous trees of Britain through the changing seasons of the year, this beautifully illustrated work covers every aspect of tree wisdom including:

- Comprehensive physical descriptions and botanical illustrations.
- The legends and myths surrounding each tree.
- Its healing powers, both for ourselves and the planet.
- Its artistic and practical uses.
- Its specific inspirational qualities.
- Its magical properties and how each features in the ancient tree alphabet.

Jacqueline Memory Paterson has lived most of her life in the West Country, developing her unique understanding through an intense relationship with Nature. She is deeply involved with alternative educative theatre, and as Archdruidess of Glastonbury she has campaigned for the right of people to worship at Stonehenge. She currently holds the Bardic Chair of Avebury.